INDUSTRY IN CLWYD

An illustrated history

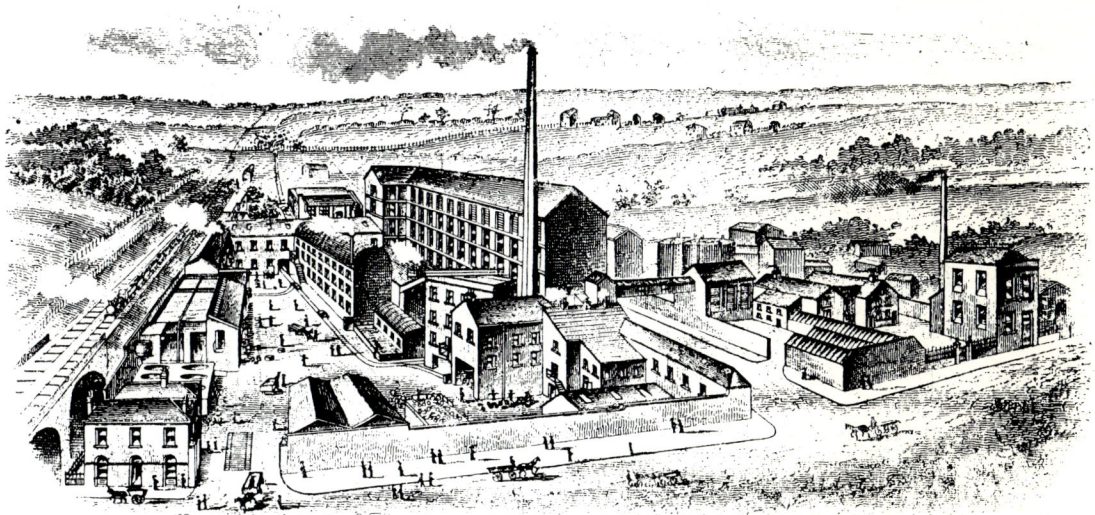

Cambrian Leather Works, Wrexham, 1893

Compiled by
C J Williams

1986

Clwyd Record Office

INDUSTRY IN CLWYD
Published by
CLWYD RECORD OFFICE
The Old Rectory, Hawarden
Deeside CH5 3NR
Designed and printed by
County Secretary's Department
Clwyd County Council

ISBN 0 903952 93 9
1986

Rhagair

gan Y Cynghorwr W. Elwyn Conway, YH
Cadeirydd Cyngor Sir Clwyd

Ers 1974 fe gyhoeddodd yr archifdy sirol gyfres o lyfrynnau darluniol ar agweddau o hanes Clwyd, y rhan fwyaf ohonynt yn ymwneud â'i threfi hanesyddol. Mae'r gyfrol hon yn ymadael â'r patrwm gan ei bod yn ymdrin â hanes diwydiant y sir ac mae'n ymddangos yn briodol iawn ym Mlwyddyn Diwydiant.

Diwydiant, ar ôl amaethyddiaeth, yw gweithgaredd hynaf a mwyaf pwysig dyn, ac mae gan ein sir orffennol diwydiannol cyfoethog. Effeithwyd arni gan y Chwyldro Diwydiannol yn gynnar a bu'n aml yn flaenllaw gyda datblygiadau newydd technolegol. Yn y blynyddoedd diwethaf cyflogai'r diwydiannau hŷn, traddodiadol, lai o bobl ac felly mae'n hanfodol bod diwydiannau newydd yn cael eu denu i'r ardal i roi'r cyfle i greu swyddi newydd. Cymer Cyngor Sir Clwyd trwy ei Adran Datblygu Economaidd ran gweithredol iawn yn y gwaith hwn. Mae Clwyd yn ardal ddeniadol iawn i ddiwydiannwyr gyda cysylltiadau da, llafurlu dawnus ac ardaloedd eang o dir diwydiannol. Wrth edrych trwy'r tudalennau hyn a darllen am waith a medrusrwydd pobl Clwyd dros nifer o ganrifoedd gobeithiwn y parha'r traddodiad yma o weithgaredd diwydiannol am amser maith.

Medi 1986

Foreword

by Councillor W. Elwyn Conway, JP
Chairman of Clwyd County Council

Since 1974, the county record office has published a series of illustrated booklets on aspects of the history of Clwyd, most of them relating to its historic towns. This volume marks a new departure, for it is concerned with the history of the county's industries, and it appears, appropriately, in Industry Year.

Industry is, after agriculture, man's oldest and most important activity, and our county has a rich industrial past. It was affected by the Industrial Revolution at an early stage, and has often been at the forefront of current technology. The older, traditional sectors of the economy have employed fewer people in recent years, and it is vital that new industries should be attracted to the area to provide new job opportunities. The county council, through its Economic Development Division, is taking a very active part in this work. Clwyd is an attractive area to the industrialist, with good communications, a skilled workforce, and large areas of industrial land. As we look through these pages, and read of the work and ingenuity of the people of Clwyd over several centuries, let us hope that this tradition of industrial activity will long continue.

September 1986

CONTENTS

Introduction

This booklet attempts to provide an outline history of the county's major industries, and to illustrate it from the record office's extensive collection of prints and photographs. No work of this kind, in such a limited space, can claim to be comprehensive. Every major industry has been included, but many long-lived concerns have been omitted, if only for lack of suitable illustrative material. The illustrations have been selected to provide as wide a geographical spread as possible and to show useful technological detail; but the history of industry is also the history of those who have worked in it, so most sections include views of people at work, as well as buildings and machinery.

It is an appropriate time, perhaps, to provide such an account, for this is a time of rapid industrial change. The area, like most coalfields with a history of mining and heavy industry in Britain and, indeed, on the continent of Europe, has seen a dramatic fall in employment in the old industries — lead and coal mining, iron and steel, and textiles. The gap is is being filled as a result of determined efforts by the county council and other authorities to attract new industry to the area. While this is a long and difficult process, it does mean that the county will never again have to rely on employment being provided by a few major industries.

The industrial revolution came early to north-east Wales. Lead and coal mines used the steam engine to pump water within a few years of its invention by Thomas Newcomen in 1712. The Greenfield valley at Holywell was an ideal site for eighteenth-century industrialists, for the water flowing from St Winefride's Well provided ample supplies to turn waterwheels and power machinery. Cotton mills were established here from 1777 onwards, and the copper and brass industries were major employers. Two men appeared on the scene who have a place in national as well as local history — Thomas Williams of Llanidan (1737-1802), the 'Copper King', a Welshman who for nearly two decades controlled the British copper industry, and the great ironmaster, John Wilkinson (1728-1808), whose Bersham works made the cylinders for the early steam engines of Boulton and Watt. The impetus came both from local landed families who devoted their energies to improving their estates, and to Englishmen who were involved as owners of capital.

Flintshire in the years 1700-50 had the fastest population growth rate in Britain (52%) and one of the fastest in 1750-1801. Considering north Wales as a whole, the concentration of industry on the coalfield of Flintshire and Denbighshire is reflected in the census statistics from 1801 onwards. Between 1801 and 1971 the population of Denbighshire increased threefold, and Flintshire over fourfold. The population of the other counties, apart from Caernarfonshire, increased far less, and that of the rural county of Montgomery actually fell slightly. There was a drift of population from agriculture to the factories of the new industrial towns and villages, a process which had its dark side; little children, many of them pauper apprentices, were forced to work long hours in cotton factories; and new villages based on coal, such as Bagillt and Rhosllanerchrugog, sprang up, in which living conditions were often described as deplorable.

The needs of industry saw the migration of skilled workers into the area. Lead mining attracted miners from Derbyshire in the eighteenth century, and from Cornwall in the nineteenth. There were strong links with Chester and, later, the great port of Liverpool. Today, the increasing mobility of labour means that thousands of people cross the border in both directions every day to go to work. In the late nineteenth and twentieth centuries such pressures have had their effect on the Welsh language, and the industrial areas close to the border became increasingly Anglicized.

In the early nineteenth century north Wales, although its industries developed, lost ground to south Wales. Here the much greater resource of coal and iron, and deep-water ports, led to a massive influx of population from other parts of Wales, and it became the dominant industrial area of the Principality. By the middle of the nineteenth century, east Denbighshire rather than Flintshire had become the centre of industrial growth, and Wrexham replaced Holywell as the largest industrial town. The population of Flintshire actually fell slightly between the censuses of 1881 and 1891. The position improved at the end of the century as new industries were established, chief among them the Summers's steelworks at Shotton. In 1901 the population of Flintshire was only 62 per cent of that of Denbighshire, but by the time of the formation of the county of Clwyd in 1974 the figures were nearly equal.

In this century industry has seen depression in the 1930s, when both counties suffered high levels of unemployment, and rapid stimulus and full employment in the war years. The two world wars brought women into many industries for the first time, and the Second World War had a lasting effect on the area. The aircraft industry, now a major employer, was established at the beginning of the war, and production at the steelworks at Brymbo, Shotton and Mostyn rose rapidly with the desperate need for steel for the war effort. Ordnance factories were built, and after the war the biggest of these, at Marchwiel, near Wrexham, became a trading estate — now the Wrexham Industrial Estate. Other industrial estates have been set up as the closure of collieries and, at Shotton recently, the steelworks, made land available for new industries. These are providing new employment to compensate for the loss of jobs in the older industries.

A constant theme in the account of many industries is the importance of communications. The canalization of the river Dee in 1733-7, and the opening of the Ellesmere Canal in 1805, stimulated industrial growth; as did, in the eighteenth century, the building of turnpike roads and, in the nineteenth, the coming of the railways. The motorway has had a similar effect, and Clwyd is at an advantage compared to some Welsh counties in its being within a few minutes' drive from the national motorway system.

In preparing this work I have been helped by many people in industry who have provided information or who have loaned illustrations, and it is striking how many industries have a strong interest in their own history. Companies provide historical notes for new members of staff, use historical material in displays and promotional publications, and include items on their organization's past story in works magazines. Awareness of and interest in the county's rich industrial past has never been greater as we enter a new industrial age.

SOURCES

A great deal of research work has been done on the history of industry in Clwyd, and much of it has been published in the journals of the two county historical societies. I have relied heavily on this work in my account of most industries, and have provided a select bibliography at the end of each section. In particular, I owe a great debt to the work of Mr Ifor Edwards and the late Mr George Lerry in the Denbighshire Historical Society's *Transactions*; and to that of Mr P.S. Richards and Dr K. Davies in the *Journal* of the Flintshire Historical Society. *Early Industry in Flintshire* (1966), by Flintshire's first county archivist, the late Mr M. Bevan-Evans, provided invaluable background. W.H. Chaloner and A.E. Musson, *Industry and Technology* (1963), is an excellent illustrated account of industry at national level, and includes a useful bibliography. My chief debt is to the late Professor A.H. Dodd, a native of Wrexham; his *The Industrial Revolution in North Wales,* first published in 1933 (and still in print), is an indispensable guide to the early history of industry in the area. Statistical background is provided by two theses: W.T.R. Pryce, 'The Social and Economic Structure of North-East Wales, 1750-1890' (PhD thesis, Lanchester Polytechnic, Coventry, 1971), and another thesis on settlement and population in Flintshire, 1801-1931, by K. Davies, published in parts in the Flintshire Historical Society's *Journal,* Vols 25-7 (1971-6); and by John Williams, *Digest of Welsh Historical Statistics* (Welsh Office, 1985). Although space has not allowed any treatment of trade unionism, its history is covered by the late Mr Emlyn Rogers in a series of articles in the Denbighshire *Transactions,* Vols 12-23 (1963-74), and Flintshire *Journal,* Vols 14-15 (1953-5).

ACKNOWLEDGEMENTS

I am grateful to the following for kindly providing illustrations and information in connection with this booklet: Aerofilms; Amalgamated Union of Engineering Workers; Mr G.A. Cantrill, Wrexham Lager Beer Co; Mr Geoffrey Charles; Mr D.P. Branigan; Central Electricity Generating Board; Mr Ifor Edwards (Acrefair Collection); Mr J.D. Edwards, Monsanto; Vicar and churchwardens of Gresford; Mr D.A. Griffin and the staff of the county council's Economic Development Division, the Information Officer, and the Director of Architecture, Planning and Estates; Sir William Gladstone; Mr E.N. Graesser; Mr J.B. Lewis; Mr S.A. Lewitt; Mrs A. Lloyd; Mr J. Glynn Morris; National Library of Wales; National Museums and Galleries on Merseyside; Karen Roden, British Aerospace; Mr J. Sandham; Mr G. Smith, British Steel Corporation; and Mr E.O.F. Williams, Brymbo Steel Works. Thanks are also due to Mrs D.M. Rowland, who typed the text, and to Barry Hamilton of the Clwyd Centre for Educational Technology, for photographic work.

Power

Water and wind

Before the eighteenth century, water and wind were the only sources of power available to industry, apart from that produced by animals and by man himself. Water mills for grinding corn were common in the Middle Ages. Over 5,000 were listed in Domesday; in the small part of present-day Clwyd listed under Cheshire there were mills at Worthenbury, Eyton, Gresford, Rhuddlan, Dyserth and Halkyn. Water mills were also used for the fulling of cloth; *pandy*, the Welsh word for a fulling mill, is still a common place-name. With the development of industry in the eighteenth century, sites in river valleys were eagerly sought after. One area in particular was suitable for the application of water power in industry — the Greenfield valley at Holywell.

Windmills were introduced into Britain about a century after the Norman Conquest. Although they mainly ground corn, they were sometimes used in industry, for example for pumping water from mines.

Steam engines

In 1712 Thomas Newcomen, a Devon engineer, set the first practical steam engine to work pumping water from a colliery near Dudley castle. Its use spread rapidly to other coalfields. One of the first engines, built by Newcomen himself, was erected at Woods mine, Ewloe, sometime between April 1714 and December 1715, and another was set to work at the Talargoch lead mine at about the same time. Both were owned by a group of Staffordshire gentlemen, who probably had a speculative interest in such engines in several mining areas. The London Lead Company, who were active in the lead-mining industry, were important early users of the steam engine. They erected seven in Flintshire between 1732 and 1762.

The Newcomen engine was a slow and inefficient device. It is properly described as an atmospheric rather than a steam engine, for it worked by admitting steam to the cylinder, and then condensing it by injecting cold water. This created a partial vacuum so that the pressure of the atmosphere forced down the piston. The engine was, however, well adapted to mine drainage, and over 1,400 were built in the course of the eighteenth century in Britain alone.

In 1769 James Watt patented his improved engine, with a separate condenser which greatly increased its efficiency. In the early years, the cylinders of the new Watt engine were made at Bersham by John Wilkinson, for only he possessed the machinery to bore the cylinder to the standard of accuracy demanded by Boulton & Watt. Unfortunately, Wilkinson began to make the engines himself, and sell these pirated versions to local mine-owners, who were thus able to avoid paying royalties to Boulton & Watt.

James Watt made other improvements to the steam engine; in the 1780s he began to use the expansive force of steam, and developed a rotary engine which could be applied to driving machinery. This freed the industrialist from the need to use water power. Machinery could now be worked anywhere where coal could be obtained to raise steam, and industry began to be concentrated in great industrial towns rather than in often remote river valleys, although it was well into the nineteenth century before the process was complete. Two local symptoms of the change were the decline of the Greenfield valley, where industry was water-powered, in the early nineteenth century, and John Wilkinson's move in the 1790s from Bersham, and water power, to Brymbo and steam power based on locally-available coal.

L.T.C. Rolt & J.S. Allen, *The Steam Engine of Thomas Newcomen* (1977)
J.N. Rhodes, 'Early Steam Engines in Flintshire', *Newcomen Society Transactions,* Vol 41 (1968-9)
Ifor Edwards, 'Some Notes on John Wilkinson and his Relations with Boulton & Watt', *Denbs Hist Soc Trans,* Vol 21 (1972)

Electricity

Before nationalization in 1948 the supply of electricity in north Wales was in the hands of a number of concerns, both private companies and local authorities. At Wrexham, in 1896, a private company had been granted an order to supply the town, but this was allowed to lapse, and the council itself built an electricity generating works in 1899. Supply began at Wrexham in 1901, and also at Colwyn Bay and Rhyl. The largest electricity undertaking in the area was the North Wales Power Co, formed in 1904, with hydro-electric stations at Cwm Dyli, on Snowdon, and later at Dolgarrog and Maentwrog. Chester had its own hydro-electric generating station, and also took over the steam generating plant built to supply the munitions factory at Queensferry during the First World War. Many private concerns, particularly collieries, had their own supplies.

The Electricity Supply Act 1926 completely re-organized the industry, and provided for the construction of the National Grid. More reliable supplies led to increasing use of electricity for power in industry. Power became available away from the traditional industrial areas on the coalfields, and helped the drift of industry to the south-east from the 1930s onwards. In north Wales, Wrexham became the headquarters of the North Wales Power Co, who built new offices at Rhostyllen in 1932.

G.G. Lerry, 'The Industries of Denbighshire from Tudor Times to the Present Day: Part III . . . Electricity Supply', *Denbs Hist Soc Trans,* Vol 9 (1960)
R.H. Morgan, 'The Development of the Electricity Supply Industry in Wales to 1919', *Welsh History Review,* Vol 11 No 3 (1983)

Rossett Mill, about 1910. The mill is dated 1661, but incorporates earlier work and later alterations. The undershot wheel drove two pairs of millstones and also worked a hoist.

CROR Photo 88/10

Drawing of a water-powered pumping engine at Sir Roger Mostyn's coal pits at Mostyn, 1684. Water from a stream turns the undershot waterwheel on the right and another higher wheel (not shown). A wooden shaft, crown-wheel and pinion (probably made by a local millwright) operate the chain-pump in the shaft in the left foreground. Rag or leather balls at intervals on the chain passed through wooden pipes, so raising the water to the surface.

Thomas Dineley, Account of the Official Progress of . . . the . . . Duke of Beaufort through Wales in 1684, *ed R.W. Banks (1888)*

The Greenfield valley at Holywell, 1792. The water which issued from St Winefride's Well ran down this wide valley for a distance of 1.5 miles to the Dee estuary, falling a distance of some 200ft in the process. The flow of water never froze in winter, and rarely flooded. These factors made the valley the best site for water-powered industry in north-east Wales, and the area developed rapidly in the late eighteenth century. Dr Johnson counted nineteen works when he visited the valley in 1774, and many large factories were built after this date.

In the foreground is the reservoir for the Battery Works, where copper goods were made. In the distance are another copper factory and a cotton mill.

CROH Print 767

A horse whim. The use of these simple devices, powered by one or more horses, was widespread in the mining industry, where they were employed to raise materials, water or men. Some of the weight was taken by the descending rope, which unwound as the other rope was wound up.

L. Simonin, Underground Life *(1869)*

Horse whim in use at the Bodfari iron mine, about 1890. This was one of a group of small haematite mines in Abergele, Bodfari, Cwm and Trelawnyd which worked up to the early years of this century. On the right is Thomas Gee, the Denbigh printer and publisher, whose family owned the mine from 1877 to 1906.

CROH Photo 7/8

11

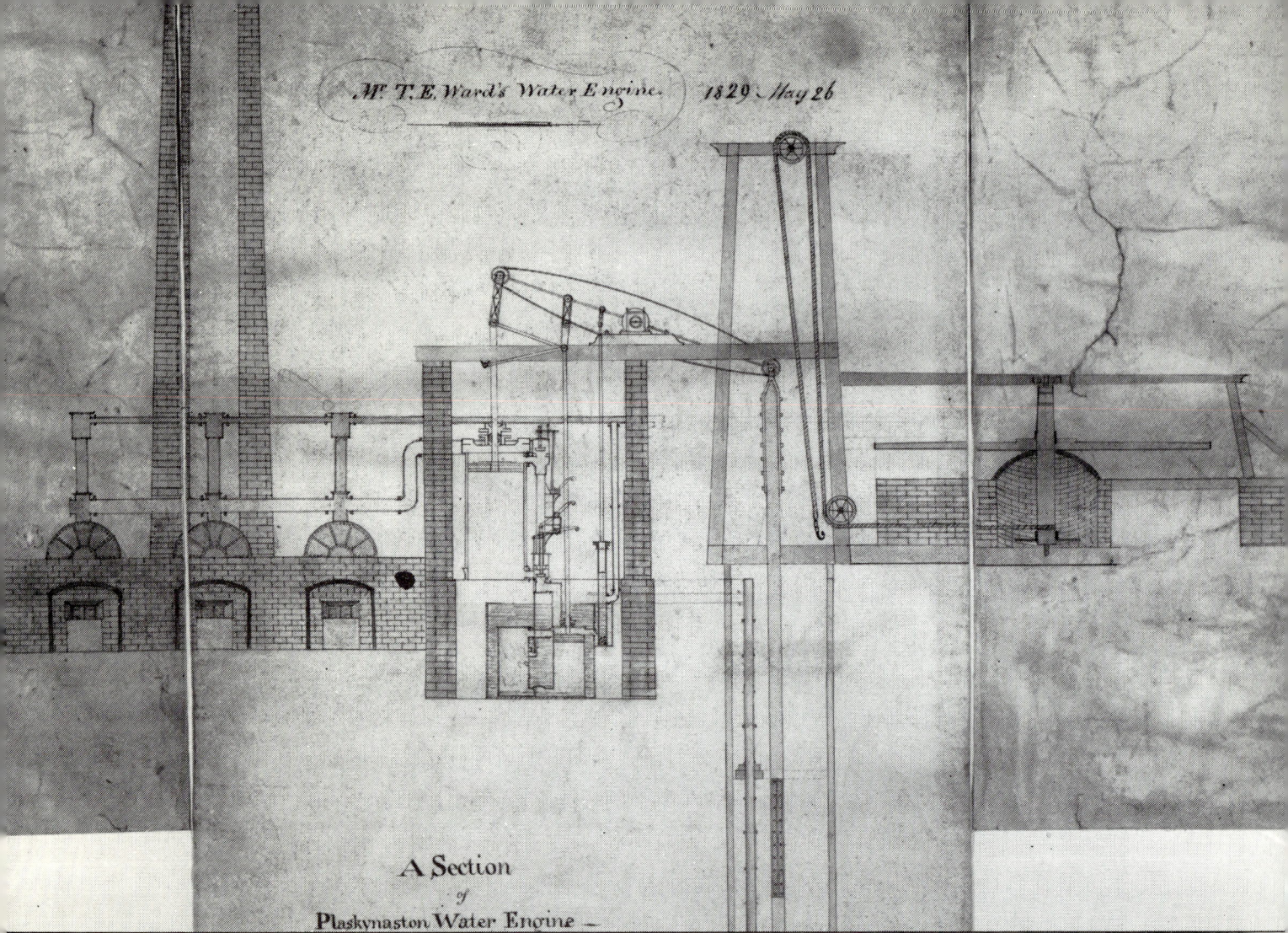

M.? T.E Ward's Water Engine. 1829 May 26

A Section
of
Plaskynaston Water Engine —

Boulton & Watt pumping engine at Plas Kynaston Colliery, Ruabon, 1829. On the left are three boilers with a steam pipe leading to the 56in cylinder, which would be enclosed in an engine-house. The steam pressure acting on the piston pulled down the beam, so raising the pump rod in the shaft. At the end of the stroke the steam exhausted into Watt's invention, the separate condenser, in a tank of water below the cylinder. The weight of the pump rod descending in the shaft worked plunger-pumps which forced a column of water up pipes in the shaft .

CROH D/DM/370

Connah's Quay power station, 1971. The building of a new power station on Deeside was proposed by Chester City Council in order to replace its existing station at Queensferry. After the nationalization of the electricity industry in 1948 it was decided that a large-scale station was needed to meet the demand for electricity in north Wales. Between 1950 and 1958 the new station was built on a site reclaimed from the Dee estuary. The six boilers and turbo-alternators had a total generating capacity of 192,000 kilowatts — equal to the demand for electricity from a city the size of Cardiff — and about 400,000 tons of coal, mostly from north Wales, were burnt each year. The station closed in 1984 (CEGB).

Lead

The lead mines of Flintshire and Denbighshire, a source of great wealth from the seventeenth to the early twentieth century, were mainly in the belt of carboniferous limestone which runs from Prestatyn, in the north-west, through Halkyn Mountain and Maeshafn to Minera in the south-east. The lead industry was developed rapidly by the Romans, who needed the metal to cover roofs and to supply water in their towns. Evidence for Roman mining in this area comes from the discovery of pigs of lead metal, dating from AD 74-96, some of them bearing the inscription 'Deceangli' (Tegeingl — later known as Englefield, Flintshire). There was a Roman smelting works at Pentre, near Flint, which was in operation from the end of the first to the middle of the second century AD.

The withdrawal of the Romans led to a decline in mining, which revived only when castles and abbeys began to be built after the Norman Conquest. During the Middle Ages the Flintshire miners, and those at Minera, worked according to traditional mining laws, administered by a barmaster. These laws were set out in the Black Prince's register in 1352, when they were granted to the miners of Hopedale. The laws did not survive beyond the Middle Ages in Denbighshire and Flintshire, although the unit of measure in them, the meer, later defined as thirty yards, remained in use until the eighteenth century.

Industrial activity increased in the Tudor period, but the mines in this area developed less rapidly than those of Cardiganshire, where the lead ore had a high silver content. The late sixteenth and early seventeenth century saw the granting of mineral rights in the Crown lordships of Bromfield and Yale in Denbighshire, and Coleshill and Rhuddlan in Flintshire — covering much of the mining area — to the Grosvenor family. The favourable economic climate after the Glorious Revolution of 1688 encouraged the mining industry. The London Lead Company, formed originally in 1692, began to work the area, and remained active until leaving in 1786 to concentrate on mines on Alston Moor in Cumberland.

The production of the Flintshire and Denbighshire lead mines between 1845, when official statistics began, and 1938, was 657,660 tons of lead ore, and 341,601 tons of zinc ore — more than any other orefield apart from the northern Pennines, and equivalent to 13 per cent of the total British production of lead ore, and 27 per cent of that of zinc. The highest output came in the 1850s and 1860s, followed by a decline, an increase in the last two decades of the century, and another decline which accelerated sharply after 1910. Before 1845 no official figures are available, but it has been estimated that in the period 1692-1845 1,870,800 tons of lead ore and 290,000 tons of zinc ore were raised: that is, over twice as much as in the years after 1845. The number of miners recorded in the census from 1841 onwards was at its highest in 1851 (2,786). Numbers tended to decline thereafter, falling to 664 in 1911. There is no evidence of numbers before 1841, although the output figures suggest that there were more miners in the eighteenth century than in the nineteenth. Even in the nineteenth century most mines were small in size. In the last quarter of the century only three mines — Minera, North Hendre and Talargoch — employed more than a hundred men for any length of time.

In the nineteenth century deep drainage levels were driven to enable mines to be worked at greater depth. The Minera mines, which had previously been worked as separate concerns, were united in 1849 into the Minera Mining Co, and a drainage level driven through the workings. At Halkyn, in 1818, the Grosvenor family drove a level, the Halkyn Deep Level, into their mines. In 1875 this was taken over by the Halkyn District Mines Drainage Co, which extended it to a length of nearly five miles, and worked a number of old mines in the process. A second drainage level was begun in 1897 at sea-level near Bagillt; this tunnel, driven by the Holywell-Halkyn Mining & Tunnel Co, drained the mines north of the Halkyn District Mines Drainage Co area, but was later extended southwards.

Mining declined in the late-nineteenth century, as bigger reserves of ore were opened up overseas, and came to an end in the early 1920s. It was revived in 1928 when Halkyn District United Mines was formed. The company was very active in the 1920s; it extended the sea-level tunnel southwards, gaining the world tunnelling record and discovering twelve new lead veins in the process. Operations were suspended during the war, but recommenced afterwards; the water emerging from the tunnel mouth was used as a water supply by Courtaulds.

W.J. Lewis, *Lead Mining in Wales* (1967)

C.J. Williams, *Metal Mines of North Wales* (1980)

C.J. Williams, 'The Lead Miners of Flintshire and Denbighshire', *Llafur — Journal of the Society for the Study of Welsh Labour History*, Vol 3 No 1 (1980)

The Llyn-y-Pandy Mine in the Alyn valley, 1796. The mine was worked at this time by the ironmaster, John Wilkinson, who had four (later six) Boulton & Watt engines to pump water. One of these was at the shaft in the foreground, and another was in the engine-house visible at Mountain Shaft, on top of the cliff (National Library of Wales).

Cathole Mine, Mold, about 1897. This beam for a pumping engine was made by the Perran Foundry of Cornwall in 1868. The photograph shows the removal of the beam, which was taken to another mine nearby.

CROH Photo 24/22

The Minera mines, about 1908. The mines were worked in the eighteenth century by, among others, a group of Chester merchants, and by John Wilkinson, and closed in 1824. In 1849 the Minera Mining Company began work. It obtained the eleven leases of the mines, and drove a deep drainage level through the workings. The company then worked very profitably for many years, raising both lead ore and zinc blende. Between 1849 and 1909 ore worth £3,250,000 was mined, and the average dividend paid up to 1897 was 30 per cent. The mine closed in 1914. Four main shafts are visible; the tall chimney on the hillside was for the smelting works.

CROR Photo 82/2

Llanfair Mine, Llanfair Talhaearn, about 1895. The 30ft waterwheel powered dressing machinery. The mine, which opened in 1890, was one of a number of smaller mines west of the Vale of Clwyd. It raised small quantities of ore until 1903.   CROR Photo 56/38

City (or Meadow) Shaft, Minera, about 1905. This shaft, 1,220ft deep, was one of the deepest in the Flintshire and Denbighshire metal mines. The engine-house, which still stands, held a 60in pumping engine, and there was a winding engine out of sight to the right.

CROR Photo 82/26

A group of Minera lead miners, about 1880.

Electric locomotive in the Milwr Tunnel in the 1930s. The tunnel, begun at sea level at Bagillt in 1897, was extended by Halkyn District United Mines, formed in 1928. The tunnel drained water from the mines, and also served as a haulage-way to the dressing plant at Pen-y-Bryn Shaft on Halkyn Mountain.

Lead smelting

In the medieval period lead was smelted in simple furnaces using dried wood and natural wind power. These furnaces, known as boles, were on hilltops, and sometimes survive as place-names — Pen-y-ball near Holywell, for example. In the seventeenth century furnaces were found in river valleys, as water power was used to work bellows. The Grosvenors' smelting mill at Mold, active in the seventeenth century, is remembered in the name Leadmill. In the 1690s coal was first used to smelt lead in a reverberatory furnace. The first such furnace to operate successfully was built by the London Lead Company at Gadlys, Bagillt, in 1703-4. Silver was refined from the lead metal; coins minted from Flintshire silver were ornamented on the reverse with a plume of feathers.

The Dee estuary soon became an important lead-smelting centre, as coal was near at hand and the lead metal could be taken out by sea. In the eighteenth century a chain of smelting works sprang up on the water's edge, at Flint, Bagillt and elsewhere. As well as smelting ore from the Denbighshire and Flintshire mines, the works obtained ore from mining areas remote from a coalfield — mid-Wales, Shropshire, Scotland, Ireland and the Isle of Man. There were a few smelting works away from the coast; Minera ore was smelted at Pentrobin, near Hawarden, from 1751 to 1810, and there were works at Minera itself for short periods. The ironmaster John Wilkinson had two smelting works with distinctive conical chimneys, one at Brymbo for Minera ore, and another at Buckley for ore from his Llyn-y-Pandy mine in the Alyn valley.

The smelting industry declined from the middle of the nineteenth century as increasing quantities of ore were imported. South Wales was better placed to deal with these, and the last Bagillt works closed in 1927.

G. Lloyd, 'The Smelt at Buckley', *Flints Hist Soc Jnl,* Vol 19 (1961)
J.N. Rhodes, 'The Lead Mills at Mold', *Flints Hist Soc Jnl,* Vol 25 (1971-2)
D.J. Rowe, *Lead Manufacturing in Britain* (1983)

Gadlys lead-smelting works, Bagillt — detail from William Williams's map of Flintshire and Denbighshire, 1720. It was at Gadlys that, in 1703-4, the London Lead Co first successfully used coal to smelt lead.

River Bank smelting-works, Bagillt — engraving from Thomas Pennant,
Whiteford and Holywell *(1796). This works was established in 1785 by the*
Macclesfield Company, which smelted lead ore and calcined calamine for
brassworks at Cheadle and Macclesfield.

Llanerch-y-môr smelting works. This was one of the smaller works on the Dee estuary. It dated from the mid-eighteenth century, and closed about 1900.

Employees of the Dee Bank smelting works, Bagillt, about 1915.

Coal

Coal has been mined in north Wales since the Middle Ages, but on a small scale before the Industrial Revolution. It was used to make lime for mortar needed in great buildings such as the royal castles of the Edwardian conquest, but peat or wood were the fuel for most people. Poor roads made coal too expensive to carry far, although coal from Ewloe was carried on pack mules to Chester, and in ships from the Mostyn area to Ireland.

Industry made little use of coal before the eighteenth century; wood was used for smelting lead and iron. From 1703, coal was used in lead-smelting, and furnaces were built on the Dee where coal was easily available. In 1709 at Coalbrookdale Abraham Darby discovered the use of coke for smelting iron, and although it took some time for the knowledge to spread, coal had largely replaced charcoal in the iron industry by the end of the eighteenth century. Coal was also the fuel used by steam engines pumping water from mines. Better transport also acted as a stimulus. The roads built by turnpike trusts in the late eighteenth and early nineteenth centuries were often made to develop a colliery area. The Ellesmere Canal, opened in 1805, linked the Denbighshire coalfield to industrial England, and the expansion of the railways in the early nineteenth century helped to increase demand. The rise of the coal industry saw the growth of the larger towns on the coalfield — Holywell, Mold, Wrexham, Ruabon — as well as new villages based on coal, such as Bagillt and Rhosllanerchrugog. Coal gas was used to light cotton factories at Mold in 1812 and Llangollen in 1820, and street lighting was introduced at Holywell in 1824 and Wrexham in 1827.

The market for coal from north Wales was mainly a local one, and in the late nineteenth century production fell further and further behind that of south Wales, which was ideally placed to supply an export market. The local pits, particularly the Flintshire ones, were small, with difficult geological problems. British coal production reached its peak of 287 million tons (more than double current output) in 1913. At this time the north Wales coalfield had 34 pits at work, mostly in Denbighshire; output was 3.3 million tons, and 14,500 miners were employed. Six collieries on the coalfield were taken over by the National Coal Board at nationalization in 1947 — Point of Ayr in Flintshire, Bersham, Llay Main, Gresford and Hafod in Denbighshire, and Ifton just over the border in Shropshire. There were then 9,300 men in the industry, and output was 2.5 million tons. Opencast mining began in 1944, initially as a wartime emergency measure, and reached a peak of 360,000 tons in 1959.

With the closure of four collieries in the period 1966-71 only Point of Ayr and Bersham remained working (although Bersham is to close during 1986). Between them they employed 1,200 men, and produced 850,000 tons of coal, most of it for the power stations at Connah's Quay and at Fidler's Ferry, near Widnes. The NCB has invested £15 million in recent years in a new drift mine at Point of Ayr, which has also been chosen as the site of a £10 million pilot plant to extract oil from coal.

K. Lloyd Gruffydd, 'Coal-mining in Flintshire during the later Middle Ages', *Flints Hist Soc Jnl,* Vol 30 (1981-2)

G.G. Lerry, *Collieries of Denbighshire,* 2nd ed (1968)

Clwyd Record Office, *Coal Mining,* Archive Teaching Unit No 3 (1975)

P.S. Richards, 'Point of Ayr Colliery: The Geology, Geography and History of a Coalmine', *Industrial Archaeology Review,* Vol 2 No 1 (1977)

Flintshire coal miners — detail from Greenvile Collins's New Exact Survey of the River Dee, *1689.*

CROH Map Collection PM/7/2

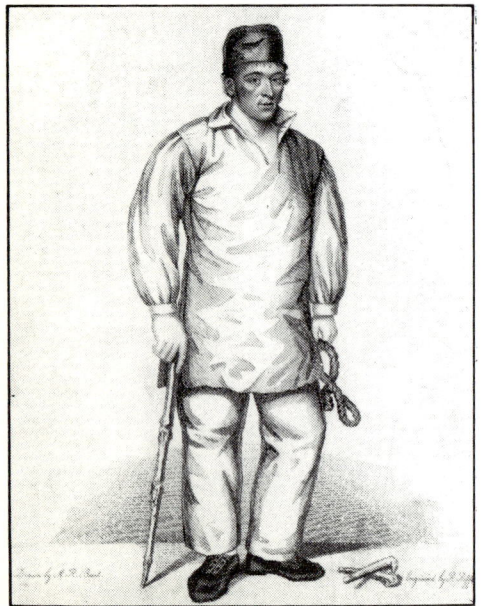

Mostyn Colliery and Ironworks, 1846. The engraved billhead shows the colliery on the left — a winding engine in the left foreground and a pumping engine and another winding engine at the water's edge. On the right is the ironworks, using coal direct from the pit. In the foreground is the newly-built Chester and Holyhead Railway, and on the embankment in the distance a horse tramway leading to Mostyn dock. The mine closed after water broke into the workings in 1884.

CROH D/DM/182/1

John Evans, a Denbighshire coal miner. This drawing of him was published after he was buried without food or light for twelve days after an accident in a pit at Minera, 1819.

CROH PR/C/38

Hafod Colliery, Rhos, about 1867. The photograph shows the colliery, sunk in 1863-7, in its early years when it was operated by the Ruabon Coal Co. In 1880, when that company went into liquidation, it was purchased by the Ruabon Coal and Coke Co. Situated near the main Wrexham-Ruabon railway line, it employed nearly 2,000 men in 1914. The colliery was one of those taken over by the National Coal Board in 1947. It closed in 1968.

CROR Photo 32/3

Plas Power Colliery, Southsea, about 1885. This colliery, sunk in 1875-7, and worked from 1877 to 1938, was one of those operated by the Broughton and Plas Power Coal Co. The company's brochure, from which this photograph is taken, claimed that its steam coal was used by many famous railway and shipping companies including Cunard, P&O, the Great Western Railway, and the Great Indian Peninsular and South Indian Railways. The company was a pioneer in the use of electricity underground, and its Plas Power and Gatewen pits were considered two of the most modern collieries in the area.

CROH D/DM/309/8

Vron Colliery, Brymbo, about 1900. Sunk about 1806, this pit was later worked for many years by Maurice & Low. (William Low was a promoter of the first Channel tunnel.) At about the time this photograph was taken it was purchased by the Broughton & Plas Power Coal Co, and used for pumping, but coal was again raised from 1914. It closed in 1930.

CROR Photo 10/50

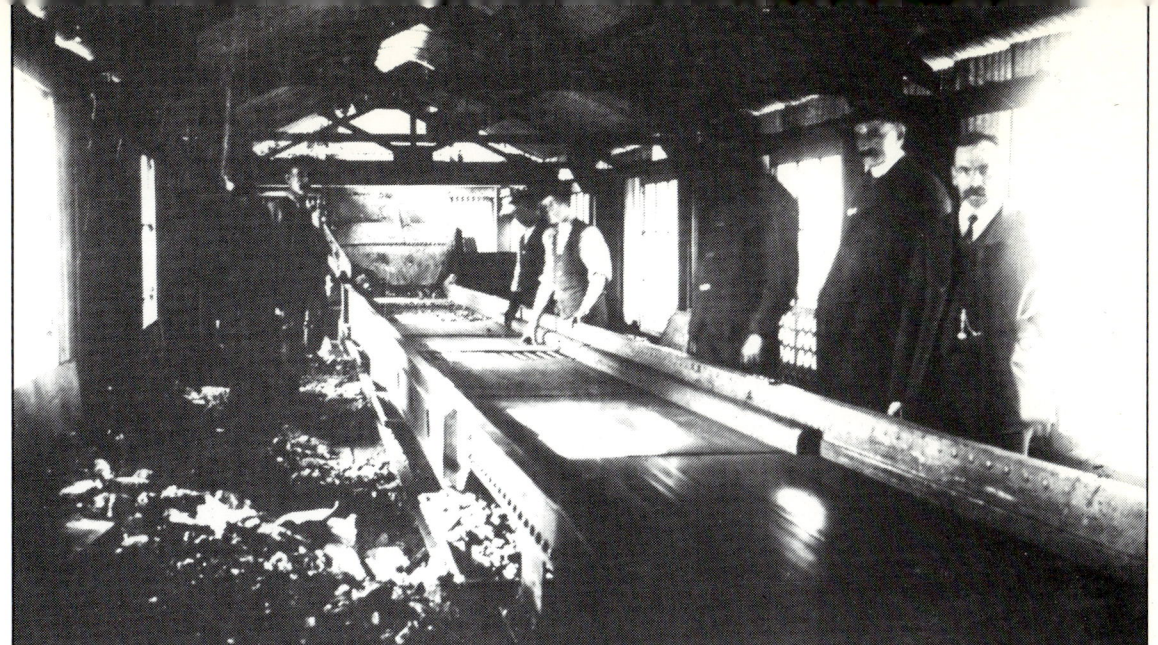

Sorting coal at Gwaith Mari, Treuddyn, about 1900.

CROH Photo 66/49

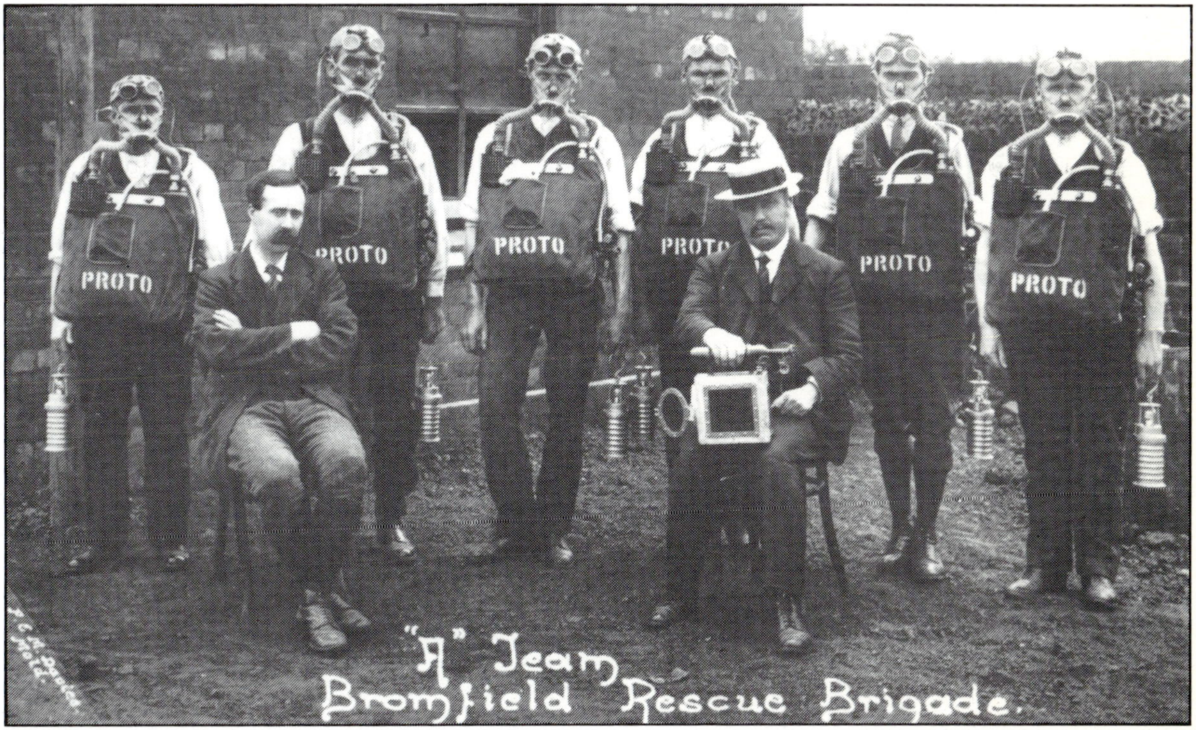

Bromfield Colliery rescue brigade, about 1920 (J. Glynn Morris).

CROH Photo 41/100

Point of Ayr Colliery, about 1910. A shaft was sunk on this site by the West Mostyn Colliery Co in 1873, but was subsequently abandoned. The mine was taken over in 1885 by Point of Ayr Collieries, and a second shaft sunk. After nationalization the pit was reorganized, and a third shaft brought into operation, in 1950-7. Until 1958 about a third of the output was loaded into small boats at the private wharf in the foreground. These boats plied between Ireland, the Isle of Man and small ports on the west coast.

CROH Photo 35/53

Office staff of Coed Talon Collieries, about 1920.

CROH Photo 66/14

Iron and Steel

The iron industry has held a central place in the industrial history of north-east Wales. There were early ironworks at Bodfari, Bersham, Chirk and Ruabon, but it was the arrival of the great ironmaster, John Wilkinson, at Bersham in 1753 which helped to stimulate the industry. A further stimulus came with the construction of the Ellesemere Canal in 1805. William Hazledine, the Shrewsbury ironmaster who made the cast-iron troughs for Pontcysyllte and Chirk aqueducts, built Plas Kynaston foundry in 1795. Thomas Jones of Gardden Hall, Ruabon (formerly of Llanerchrugog Hall, Rhos) worked Ponciau forge about 1807, opened Llwynennion ironworks by 1811, and from 1819 built furnaces at Leeswood and Coed Talon which worked until 1867. The Ponciau works was leased in 1813 by James Thompson, who worked at Brymbo for a time, and at the Ffrwd ironworks from about 1824.

In the Ruabon area the leading ironmaster was Edward Rowland. In 1825 his son, Edward Lloyd Rowland, sold his estate and the Acrefair ironworks to the British Iron Company, a firm with extensive works at Abersychan, Monmouthshire, and Corngreaves, Staffs. The company and their successors, the New British Iron Company, worked up to 1888. At Hawarden, an ironworks was operated from the 1770s to 1844 by the Rigby family, who made cannon, iron bridges and boilers.

After the 1820s, as production was concentrated into larger units, many of the smaller ironworks in this area closed. The industry lost ground to that of south Wales, particularly as ore was imported in increasing quantities, making access to a port an important factor. The Mostyn and Shotton works were developed on the Dee estuary, and Brymbo survived by turning to the production of high-quality special steel.

Bersham

Bersham ironworks, built about 1670, was operated in the early eighteenth century by the Quaker, Charles Lloyd of Dolobran. In 1721 Lloyd successfully used coke in place of charcoal for smelting iron at Bersham, as his friend Abraham Darby had done at Coalbrookdale in 1709. The works was leased in 1753 to Isaac Wilkinson, a Lancashire man attracted by its water power and resources of coal and ironstone. From 1763 the works was operated by his elder son, John Wilkinson (1728-1808), who had established furnaces and foundries at New Willey, near Broseley in Shropshire (1756), and at Bradley near Bilston in Staffordshire (1758).

At Bersham great quantities of armaments were made in the closing years of the Seven Years War (1756-63). Wilkinson experimented with, and later patented, machinery for the boring of cannon. This had important consequences when in 1775 Boulton and Watt began to make James Watt's improved steam engines. Only John Wilkinson could bore the cylinders to the required standard of accuracy, and he supplied them to Boulton and Watt for twenty years (see Engineering). The arrangement came to an end when it was discovered that Wilkinson had been making pirated engines incorporating Watt's improvements, and selling them locally. Wilkinson also quarrelled violently with his partner, his brother William. This resulted about 1793 in the partial destruction of much of the works, which then lay idle until they were sold off after the elder brother's death.

Brymbo

In 1792 John Wilkinson bought the Brymbo Hall estate, and there built a new ironworks. Water power was no longer essential, as it could be replaced by rotative steam engines, so the reserves of coal and ironstone made Brymbo a better site than Bersham. Here one of the early furnaces, Old Number One, rebuilt in 1818 and in use until 1894, still stands in what is now Brymbo steelworks.

The Scottish engineer, Henry Robertson (1816-88), was engaged by Scottish banks to investigate the industrial potential of north-east Wales. His report led them to invest large sums in the development of mineral railways from about 1840. Henry Robertson also partnered Robert Roy in the new development of the Brymbo ironworks, and completely revitalized it. By 1846 Roy left, and the new Brymbo company was placed in the charge of W.H. Darby and C.E. Darby, of the famous Coalbrookdale family of ironmasters. The Darbys, a Quaker family, established schools and provided a workers' institute, and were active in the local community.

In 1884 Henry Robertson founded the Brymbo Steel Company, and in the following year produced the first steel in Britain to be made by the basic open-hearth process. The first sales were to the Alyn Tinplate Co at Mold. The works closed down in the great depression, for the years 1931 to 1933, but during the Second World War, because of its isolated position, it was selected to supply the aircraft industry, and has since concentrated on the production of high-quality steels. An electric melting shop to replace the old basic open-hearth furnaces was built in 1959. In recent years a £65 million investment programme has made the works, which now employs about 1,200 people, a market leader in the production of special steel for the engineering and motor industries.

Shotton

John Summers, the founder of the firm of John Summers & Sons, owned in 1842 a workshop making clogs in Dukinfield, Cheshire. In 1851, after a visit to the Great Exhibition, he bought a machine for making nails. Shortly afterwards he purchased an old engineering business in Stalybridge, and made it into a full iron and steel works, the Globe Ironworks.

In 1896 the firm was attracted to Shotton, an extensive flat site on a navigable river with supplies of coal and bricks nearby, and access by rail to the port of Liverpool. The works made steel sheet, producing 600 tons a week in early years. Imported steel bars were used until the first steelworks — ten open-hearth furnaces and a bar mill — was opened in 1902. In 1908 Shotton became the firm's head office, and in 1910 Garden City was built to house its workers.

Output doubled during the First World War with a second steelworks opening in 1917, and production was stimulated in the 1920s by the growth of the motor industry. In 1939 a continuous strip rolling mill was built, supplied by the Mesta Machine Co of Pittsburgh. Over two million tons of steel were made for the war effort in the Second World War. Blast furnaces and a new steelworks, opened in 1953, made Shotton a fully-integrated works for the first time. At its peak, the works employed over 13,000 people.

Pig iron was at first shipped in on the River Dee, and later iron ore was transported by rail to Shotton from the port of Bidston. Escalating production costs and a world-wide surplus of steelmaking capacity led to the closure of iron- and steel-making at Shotton in 1980, and the loss of 8,000 jobs had a most serious effect on the local economy. Shotton is now a cold rolling and strip coating centre — one of the most modern in the world — employing 2,200 people. A new coatings department, opened in 1979, and subsequently extended, accommodates four large coil coating lines, representing an investment of over £75 million.

I. Edwards, 'The Charcoal Iron Industry of East Denbighshire 1630-90', *Denbs Hist Soc Trans*, Vol 9 (1960)
'The Charcoal Iron Industry of Denbighshire', *Denbs Hist Soc Trans*, Vol 10 (1961)
'Iron Production in North Wales: the Canal Era: 1795-1850', *Denbs Hist Soc Trans*, Vol 14 (1965)
'The British Iron Co', *Denbs Hist Soc Trans*, Vol 31 (1982)
'The New British Iron Co', *Denbs Hist Soc Trans*, Vol 32 (1983)
A.N. Palmer, *John Wilkinson and the Old Bersham Iron Works* (1899)
W.H. Chaloner, *People and Industries* (1963). (Chapter 2: John Wilkinson)
P.S. Richards, 'The Darwen & Mostyn Iron Company', *Flints Hist Soc Jnl*, Vol 24 (1969-70)
'The Hawarden Bridge . . . Iron and Steel Works of Messrs John Summers & Co', *Flints Hist Soc Jnl*, Vol 25 (1971-2)
British Steel Corporation, *Full Circle: The Story of Steelmaking on Deeside* (1980)
Luther Griffiths, 'Brymbo and its Industry' (unpublished MS: copy in CRO) (1958)

John Wilkinson's Bersham ironworks in the late eighteenth century.

A.N. Palmer, John Wilkinson and the Old Bersham Ironworks *(1899).*

▲ *Brymbo Ironworks, about 1860.*

CROR Photo 10/37

▼ *Brymbo Steelworks, about 1930.*

CROR Photo 10/41

Repair shop at the blast pits (known as the Waterloo shop), Brymbo, about 1860.

CROR Photo 10/51

A John Wilkinson halfpenny trade token, 1793.

Brymbo Steelworks, 1893.

CROR Photo 10/34

Brymbo furnace crew, 1949 (G. Charles)

CROR DD/DM/73/4

Mostyn Ironworks, about 1908. An ironworks and colliery were established here by the Mostyn Coal and Iron Co in the early nineteenth century. The site was a favourable one, for supplies of coal and ironstone were close at hand, and in the late 1840s the Chester and Holyhead Railway was built within a few yards of the works. Iron ore was later imported through Mostyn dock, nearby. In 1887 the Darwen & Mostyn Iron Co took over and extended the works, which concentrated on the production of ferro-manganese. It closed in 1964.

CROH Photo 42/67

JOHN SUMMERS & SONS LIMITED

Globe Iron Works, Stalybridge, covering 12 acres.

Hawarden Bridge Works, Shotton covering 60 acres.

MANUFACTURERS OF

GALVANIZED, CORRUGATED & PLAIN SHEETS,
STEEL NAIL STRIPS & SHEETS, HOOPS, CUT NAILS, TACKS, &c.

LIVERPOOL OFFICE, 14 CHAPEL STREET.

MANCHESTER OFFICE, 33 BRAZENNOSE STREET.

GLOBE IRON WORKS, STALYBRIDGE.

HAWARDEN BRIDGE STEEL WORKS,
AS/ SHOTTON, FLINTSHIRE

▲ Letterhead of John Summers & Sons, showing the Stalybridge and Shotton works, 1908.

CROH DC/68

▼ General view of the Shotton works, with the head office in the left foreground, about 1930.

CROH Photo 62/62

Bar mills, No 1 Steelworks, Shotton, about 1902.

CROH D/DM/895/2

Galvanizing department packing shop, Shotton, 1910.

CROH D/BJ/444

Open-hearth furnaces, No 1 Steelworks, Shotton, about 1920.

CROH D/DM/895/2

Ships at Summers' jetty, about 1910.

CROH Photo 62/56

Casting ingots, No 2 Steelworks, Shotton, 1940.

CROH D/DM/895/2

Copper

Copper goods were manufactured in the Greenfield valley from the 1730s, but the industry reached its height after 1780, when Thomas Williams of Llanidan set up works at the lower end of the valley to process copper from the mines on Parys Mountain in Anglesey. After smelting at Ravenhead in Lancashire (later at Amlwch) the metal was taken by sea to Holywell. Here there was a rolling mill, copper forge and wire mill. The most important product was copper sheathing for ships' bottoms, but small articles were also made for the African slave trade.

In 1785 Thomas Williams acquired an interest in the second great mine on Parys Mountain, the Mona Mine. (This enabled him to control the British copper industry for the next two decades, so that he became known as the Copper King.) At the same time he took over a brass-battery mill in the Greenfield valley, where in 1787 he built a new rolling-mill to manufacture brass plate, utensils and wire.

After the death of Thomas Williams in 1802 some of his Holywell works were taken over by one of his associates, Pascoe Grenfell, whose main interests lay in the copper industry in Swansea. The Anglesey mines declined after Williams's death, and Swansea, which was in a better position to smelt ore from the Cornish mines, developed at the expense of Holywell. Some of the works at Holywell were acquired by Newton Lyons & Co (later Newton Keates), who worked them until final closure in 1894.

J. R. Harris, *The Copper King* (1964)
K. Davies & C.J. Williams, *The Greenfield Valley,* 2nd ed (1986)

Battery works, Greenfield, 1796. Waterwheels on this site powered hammers to shape copper pans, bowls, etc. In 1786 the works was sold to Thomas Williams's Greenfield Copper and Brass Co. Another of the company's factories — Meadow Mill, in the background — produced copper sheathing for ships.

CROH Print 765

Greenfield brass mills, 1792. Here small copper articles were made for the African slave trade. After 1785, when it was taken over by the Greenfield Copper & Brass Co, the works specialized in the production of brass ingots and plate.

CROH Print 720

Textiles

Holywell

The cotton-spinning industry at Holywell was founded in 1777 by John Smalley, a former associate of Richard Arkwright at Preston and Nottingham. In partnership with John Chambers of Holywell he built the Yellow Mill, powered by the stream issuing from St Winefride's Well. In the boom years of the 1780s new mills were built, the Upper Mill (1783), the Lower Mill (1785), and Crescent Mill (1790). The works were described in some detail by Thomas Pennant in his *History of . . . Whiteford and Holywell* (1796). The Cotton Twist Company then had over 1,225 employees, including some three hundred apprentices, many of them poor boys sent to work at the mills to save them being a burden on the rates.

The industry suffered a slump in trade in 1837. Although steam power had been introduced, the Holywell company could not compete with the Lancashire mills, and went into liquidation about 1841. In 1848 the Crescent Mill was taken over by a Newtown man, Thomas Jones, who set up a power loom (the first in Wales) to weave flannel. A new company, the Welsh Flannel Manufacturing Company, was formed to work both the Crescent and Upper Mills. This was a partnership of William Brown (of Brown's of Chester), who provided the capital, and Urias Bromley, who provided the technical knowledge. Thomas H. Waterhouse, a Yorkshire man, joined the company in 1874, and later succeeded Bromley as manager. He himself was succeeded in 1902 by his son Thomas Waterhouse, who guided the mill through a major modernization, the slump of the 1920s, and expansion after 1946. A private investment company acquired the mill in 1957, which has adapted to changing fashions, and three quarters of its output of yarn is now exported to Japan, the USA, West Germany and France. The company are specialists in producing yarns from natural fibres in natural colours, and are now the oldest woollen manufacturing company in England and Wales.

Mold

Following the early success at Holywell, a mill was built on the river Alyn in Mold in 1792. It was greatly enlarged in the boom year of 1825, but closed for a short period in the 1830s; after re-opening it turned to weaving as well as spinning. In 1866 it was burned down, and as trade had not recovered from the shortage of cotton during the American Civil War, did not re-open.

Llangollen

Two textile mills have been worked in Llangollen. The older, the Lower Dee Mills, beside the river Dee, was opened in 1805 by two Manchester men, William Turner and Andrew Comber. The attraction of Llangollen as a site was the availability of water power, and also the recently completed canal. Unlike the Holywell concerns, where only spinning was done, both spinning and weaving were carried out at Llangollen, and finished goods produced. This was one of the first mills at which power looms were employed. The mills were rebuilt in 1815, after a disastrous fire, but in 1819 Turner & Comber went bankrupt, and the factory lay idle for several years until it was bought in 1824 by another Manchester firm. Like Holywell, it closed during the slump of the 1830s; it was converted to the production of flannel and woollens, and blankets were made up to 1967. A second woollen mill, the Upper Dee Mills, built in 1855, went out of production about 1920.

E.J. Foulkes, 'The Cotton-Spinning Factories of Flintshire, 1777-1866', *Flints Hist Soc Jnl,* Vol 21 (1964)

P.S. Richards, 'The Holywell Textile Mills, Flintshire', *Industrial Archaeology,* Vol 6 No 1 (1969)

K. Davies & C.J. Williams, *The Greenfield Valley,* 2nd ed (1986)

Ifor Edwards *et al,* 'Industry at Llangollen', *Denbs Hist Soc Trans,* Vol 18 (1969)

Cotton mills in the Greenfield valley, Holywell, 1796. In the foreground is the Upper Mill (1783). According to Thomas Pennant, this six-storied factory took only six weeks to build; its 198 windows lit up the neighbourhood at night. The Crescent Mill, lower down, was built in 1790.

CROH Print 766

Holywell textile mills, about 1910 (J. Sandham).

The Welsh Flannel Manufacturing Co mills at Holywell, 1911.

CROH Photo 30/38

Mold cotton mill, as depicted on a creamware jug, 1792 (National Museums and Galleries on Merseyside).

CROH Photo 40/301

45

Lleweni bleachworks 'as at first intended to be built', 1792. This remarkable building, which cost over £20,000, was constructed about 1780 by Thomas FitzMaurice, who had recently bought the Lleweni estate. Some 4,000 pieces of linen were sent over each year by his Irish tenants in payment of rents. Much was also sent from neighbouring counties for bleaching. Walter Davies, in his General View of the Agriculture and Domestic Economy of North Wales *(1810), compared Thomas FitzMaurice favourably with those of the Welsh gentry who neglected agriculture and industry in favour of genealogy. 'He thought he derived more true honour from the words "Ballymote Manufacture", the inscription over his linen-shop in Chester, than from the most pompous motto, in French or Latin, upon his escutcheon.'*

CROR Print 303

Workers at Llangollen woollen mill, about 1880 (National Library of Wales).

Brewing and Mineral Water

Brewing has been an important industry in Wrexham since the seventeenth century. At one time it had nine breweries, but most other towns had at least one. The demand for malt, the basic raw ingredient, explains the large number of maltsters listed in early nineteenth-century directories. Much brewing was carried out in small brewhouses attached to inns or large houses, but A.N. Palmer dates the first brewery in Wrexham not connected to a public house to 1799. This was in College Street, on a site later occupied by the Albion brewery.

Mineral water has been made at a number of places in Clwyd, including Wrexham (J.F. Edisbury & Co and the Zoedone Co), Ruthin (R. Ellis & Son and Cambrian Mineral Waters) and Holywell (W. Hall & Son).

G.G. Lerry, 'The Industries of Denbighshire from Tudor Times to the Present Day: Part III(b) — the Breweries of Wrexham', *Denbs Hist Soc Trans*, Vol 9 (1960)

P.F. Mason, 'Castle Hill Brewery, Ewloe', *Annual Report of the County Archivist*, 1979

Brewery workers, about 1910 (Wrexham Lager Beer Co)

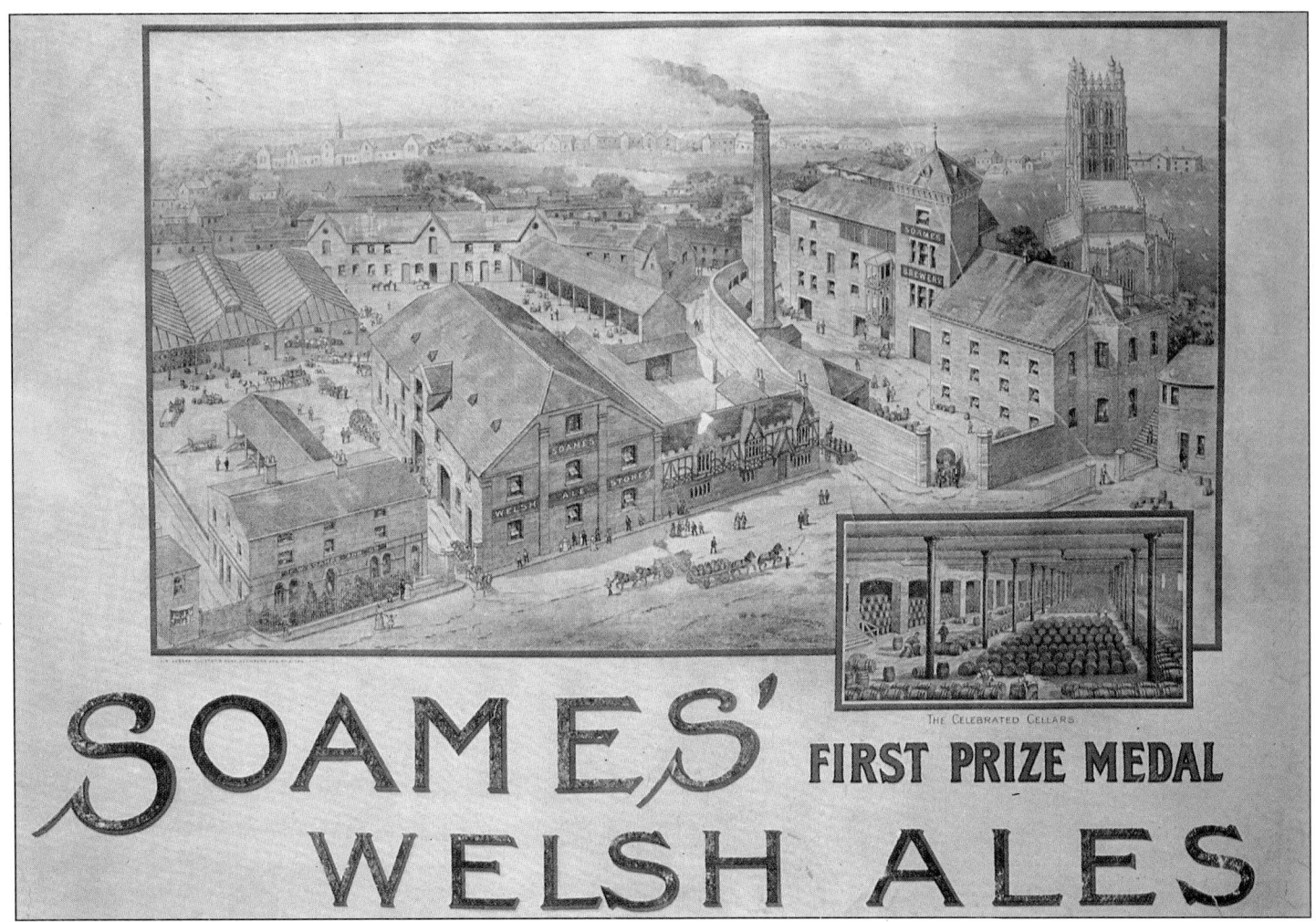

Soames's brewery, Wrexham, about 1880. This illustration dates from soon after 1879, when the brewery was purchased by F.W. Soames and rebuilt and extensively modernized. In 1931 F.W. Soames & Co amalgamated with Huntley & Mowat (the Island Green brewery, Pentrefelin) and Dorsett Owen & Co of Oswestry to form Border Breweries.

CROR DD/DM/104

Wrexham Lager Beer Co advertisement, about 1900. The first lager brewery was built in Wrexham in 1882, and taken over in 1886 by R.F. Graesser, a German chemical manufacturer (see Chemicals). The company found it difficult to break into local markets; only in 1922 did it acquire its first pub in Wrexham. Early sales were to hotels and clubs, and to great shipping lines such as Cunard and White Star, who found that the lager kept well on their ships. Then as now, Wrexham lager was exported (from Wrexham, England!) to all parts of the world. The brewery, now owned by Allied Lyons, is one of the most modern in Europe.

CROR DD/DM/456/1

The Wrexham Lager Brewery, about 1930 (Wrexham Lager Beer Co)

Castle Hill Brewery, Ewloe — the bottling room, about 1930. The brewery, run by the Fox family from 1844 to 1948, supplied a network of public houses on Deeside and in the Hawarden, Buckley and Mold areas.

CROH Photo 18/81

Ellis's mineral water works, Ruthin, 1907. The firm of R. Ellis & Son was established in Ruthin in 1825. At the turn of the century its range of products included soda and tonic water, ginger ale, lemonade and seltzer water.

Ruthin Pocket Guide, *1908*

The packing room at the Cambrian works of the Ruthin Soda Water Co, about 1900.

CROR Photo 90/178

Chemicals

At Acrefair Graessers and Monsanto, and at Flint and Greenfield Courtaulds made this area an important centre of the chemical industry. At Flint in 1852 the firm of Muspratt & Huntley established an alkali works on the site of the old lead-smelting works beside Flint Castle. (James Muspratt, a pioneer of alkali manufacture in Lancashire, had started a works at St Helens in 1828.) Muspratts (later the United Alkali Co) were followed by Smith & Mawdsley at the Pentre alkali works, Flint. Other smaller chemical works were at Connah's Quay, Queensferry and Prestatyn.

Courtaulds

The manufacture of synthetic fibre on Deeside had its origins in Lloyd George's Patent Act of 1907, which required those with British patents to work them within three years. This led the German Glanzstoff Company, the largest manufacturers of artificial silk, to open the Aber works at Flint in 1908. British Glanzstoff began work in 1910, using the cuprammonium process. The reasons for the choice of Flint, apart from good communications, included a plentiful supply of clean water from the Halkyn lead mines, and the

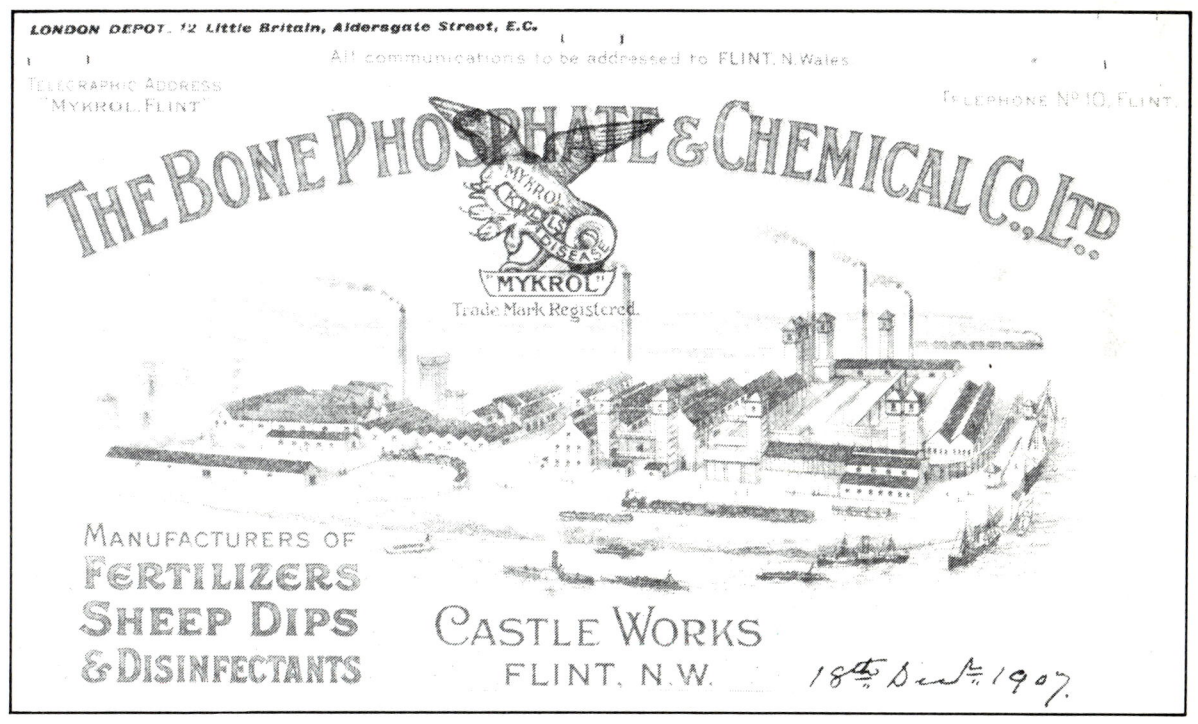

Castle Works, Flint, 1907. Part of the premises was then occupied by the Bone Phosphate & Chemical Co as under-lessees of the United Alkali Co, who held the main works. After allowance is made for some artistic licence, the billhead gives a good impression of this extensive complex on the Dee estuary, with the Chester-Holyhead railway line in the background.

CROH D/DM/888/12

R.F. Graesser

D/DM/311/31

Graessers and Monsanto

The foundation of the chemical industry at Acrefair was laid by Robert Ferdinand Graesser, born in Saxony, Germany. He came to England in 1863 at the age of nineteen and worked as a chemist, later being in charge of phenol production in the Manchester laboratory of Dr F. Crace Calvert. Phenol was largely used in medicine; this was the period when the great surgeon, Joseph Lister, was demonstrating the use of carbolic as an antiseptic.

In partnership with a Manchester lawyer, Timothy Crowther, Graesser set up a works at Acrefair in 1867 to produce paraffin from the shale waste from local collieries, but within a few years the newly-discovered oil wells in the USA lowered the price and made the business uneconomic. His partnership with Crowther now dissolved, Graesser turned to the production of phenol from crude carbolic produced by the expanding gas and tar industries. Production, less than 25 tons before 1870, rose to 200 tons by 1875, and by 1910 Graessers was producing half the world supply. Through family connections with textile manufacturing in Saxony, Graesser took an interest in the production of synthetic dyes, and later produced picric acid for the treatment of burns. At the outbreak of the First World War his works was the largest non-ordnance factory to produce picric acid for explosives.

In 1920 a half share in Graessers was acquired by the Monsanto Chemical Co of St Louis, Missouri. Founded in 1901 by John Francis Queeny, it was named after his wife, Olga Monsanto. The field of production at Cefn was widened by the introduction of new lines including saccharin, vanillin, salicylic acid and aspirin. In 1928 the partnership with Graessers ended. N.H. Graesser undertook not to compete for five years; in 1934 he erected a new tar acid refining plant at Sandycroft. The business continued to trade as R. Graesser Ltd until 1971, but the names survives in Graesser Laboratories Ltd.

Monsanto manufactured its first rubber chemicals at Cefn in 1930. Production increased during the Second World War, with materials for armaments, textiles, food and pharmaceuticals, and by 1946 200 products were made. The plant is now the main European manufacturing centre for Monsanto's range of specialized industrial chemicals. About 540 people are employed, and some 40,000 tonnes of chemical products are made each year, over eighty per cent being for export.

H. Taylor, *Historic Notices . . . of Flint* (1883)

P.S. Richards, 'Viscose Rayon Manufacture on Deeside', *Flints Hist Soc Jnl*, Vol 23 (1967-8)

CROH D/DM/311 Records of R. Graesser Ltd, 1871-1967, including centenary brochure, 1967

G.G. Lerry, 'The Industries of Denbighshire . . . Part III(a) — Chemicals', *Denbs Hist Soc Trans*, Vol 8 (1959)

I. Edwards, 'History of the Monsanto Chemical Works Site, Cefn Mawr . . *Denbs Hist Soc Trans*, Vol 16 (1967)

availability of labour accustomed to work in the chemical industry, for the United Alkali Co were withdrawing from the area and concentrating on their Lancashire and Cheshire factories.

In 1913 the Flint works, by agreement with Samuel Courtauld & Co, changed to their superior viscose process. In the following year, with the outbreak of war, British Glanzstoff closed on account of its German connections, and eventually went into liquidation. It was taken over by Courtaulds in 1917. Originally silk weavers, they had pioneered the production of viscose rayon yarn at Coventry in the early years of the century.

After the First World War Courtaulds began to extend their factories. In 1920 they bought the United Alkali Co works to the west of Flint Castle and built a new factory for spinning yarn — Castle Works. The third Courtaulds factory in Flint, Deeside Mill, purchased in 1927, was originally a small experimental cotton spinning plant to develop Fibro, the trade name for viscose rayon staple. (Rayon is produced from imported wood pulp, broken down into cellulose.) A boom in demand for consumer goods during the 1920s led to the building of a new factory, Greenfield Works, opened in 1934, to produce twenty million pounds of Fibro a year. By 1937 the factory was producing to capacity, and was extended so that output reached fifty million pounds. After the war a chemical works was built to produce sulphuric acid. The Courtaulds factories on Deeside meant that the area became the most important centre for the production of rayon in Britain. Until recent closures, Courtaulds were major employers of labour; the four factories employed 5,200 people, 1,300 of them women and girls.

Courtaulds' Flint factories, about 1960. Adjoining Flint Castle is Castle Works (on the site of the old lead-smelting works), and behind it, on opposite sides of the main road and railway, Deeside Mill and Aber Works (Aerofilms).

CROH Photo 20/40

Part of Courtaulds' Aber Works, about 1965.

CROH D/DM/340/130

Employees at Graesser's chemical works, 1879. The firm had 29 men at this time; a few of those in the photograph were from the nearby ironworks or boatmen from the canal (Monsanto).

One of the laboratories at Graesser-Monsanto (as the firm was known in the years 1920-8), 1923 (Monsanto).

The phenol plant at Graesser-Monsanto, 1924 (Monsanto).

Quarrying

Quarrying in north-east Wales was confined mainly to building stone until the eighteenth century. The industrial revolution saw a period of rapid expansion as demand rose for building stone and lime for mortar, and lime was also used in agriculture and as a flux in the iron industry. Most quarries were small and served a local market, as transport costs were high. Improved roads, the Ellesmere canal, and the coming of the railways brought access to a wider market. On the coast, the limestone quarries sent building stone and mortar by sea to Liverpool. There were slate and slab quarries around Llangollen, Corwen and Glynceiriog, but these were of minor importance compared to the great slate quarries of Caernarfonshire and Merioneth.

In 1858 there were twelve quarries in Flintshire and twenty-eight in Denbighshire, but this undoubtedly excludes some small producers. Total output (mostly of limestone) amounted to over 430,000 tons, the Minera quarries being the biggest producers with 165,000 tons. As well as being used in building, agriculture and the iron and chemical industries, limestone was used for making cement, and was supplied to the Staffordshire potteries.

Production of limestone has increased enormously since the Second World War, with most of the increase coming from the demand for aggregates in the construction industry, and particularly in road-building. In the early 1950s there were twenty-nine quarries in Flintshire and Denbighshire, producing 1,370,000 tons of limestone. Over the last thirty years there has been a trend towards fewer and bigger quarries; sixteen are now at work. Production rose to a peak of 6.5 million metric tonnes in 1973, but declined to 4.5 million in 1981. It is now in the region of 6 million tonnes. High quality limestone is used in the chemical and pharmaceutical industries, and in the manufacture of glass, plastics, pottery, rubber and ceramics.

E. Neaverson, 'Medieval Quarrying in North-Eastern Wales', *Flints Hist Soc Jnl,* Vol 14 (1953-4)

G.G. Lerry, 'The Industries of Denbighshire from Tudor Times to the Present Day: Part II — the Extractive Industries: Stone Quarrying', *Denbs Hist Soc Trans,* Vol 7 (1958)

Glyn Davies, *Minera* (1964) [pp 37-50 on limestone quarrying]

B. Jones & M. Rawcliffe, *Llanddulas: Heritage of a Village* (1985) [pp 32-51 on limestone quarrying]

Mineral Statistics of the United Kingdom . . ., Part II for 1858 (1860)

Ifor Edwards, 'Slate Quarries in the Llangollen District', *Denbs Hist Soc Trans,* Vol 34 (1985)

Mineral Working in Clwyd: Clwyd County Minerals Local Plan: Final Draft Written Statement (Clwyd County Council, 1982) [CROH CC/P/3/24]

30ft waterwheel powering planing and sawing machinery at the Deeside slate works, Glyndyfrdwy, about 1900.

CROR Photo 104A/21

Llangynhafal quarry, 1906. Such hand methods, with simple machinery powered by a traction engine, must have been typical of many small quarries at the turn of the century.

CROR Photo 67/3

Kneeshaw Lupton's limestone quarries, Llysfaen, about 1880. An incline behind the Hoffman kiln ran down to a jetty on the shore (National Library of Wales).

CROR Photo 51/35

Minera Lime Co works, Minera, about 1910. In the background are the chimneys of the Hoffman kilns, erected in 1868 and 1874.

CROR Photo 82/1

Pandy granite quarry, Glyntraean, with the Glyn Valley Tramway in the foreground, 1899. The illustration is from the catalogue of Thomas Larmuth & Co of Salford, whose Hirnant rock drills were used by the Ceiriog Granite Co at this quarry. CROH D/DM/244/15

Halkyn & Hendre Lime Co works, Hendre, 1931. This drawing by W.L. Lloyd (son of the quarry manager) shows the kiln in the background, with boiler house and locomotive shed on the left (Mrs A. Lloyd).

CROH PR/A/28 ▼

Paper and Printing

Before the late-seventeenth century, most of the paper used in Britain was imported from the continent. The basic needs of the industry were considerable quantities of clean water and a supply of linen rags, so paper mills were usually on a river near a large town. From the 1650s there are references to paper mills at work in or near Wrexham, some of which were on the river Clywedog. Mills were established at Halghton by 1706, in the Greenfield valley before 1744, and on the river Wheeler at Afonwen in 1786.

In the nineteenth century there were three paper mills on the Clywedog in Bersham and Esclusham, which between them employed eighty-four people in 1841. One of these, the Turkey Mill, was acquired in 1854 by H.M. Greville, who specialized in the making of banknote and cheque papers until the mill was burned down in 1897. It was re-opened, and worked for a time by the proprietors of Afonwen mill, but closed about 1914. Afonwen produced hand-made writing and ledger paper until 1918.

A mill at the lower end of the Greenfield valley was taken over in 1854 by the London firm of Grosvenor, Chater & Co. This firm made fine stationery and printing papers, initially from rags, jute and hessian, but from the 1860s imported esparto grass from north Africa was used. It closed in 1982. The North Wales Paper Mill was established at Oakenholt by McCorquodales, a famous Liverpool paper firm, in 1870. This specialized in the making of news, white and coloured printings, and soon turned to the use of chemical wood pulp.

The most recent arrival on the scene is the new paper mill at Shotton, opened by the Prince of Wales in December 1985. United Paper Mills has invested over £100 million in this new plant which will eventually employ some 250 people and produce about 550 tonnes of paper a day from British wood pulp.

A.E. Davies, 'Paper-Mills and Paper-Makers in Wales 1700-1900', *National Library of Wales Journal,* Vol 15 (1967-8)

M.C. Powell, 'The Paper Industry of the River Clywedog', *Denbs Hist Soc Trans,* Vol 34 (1985)

P.S. Richards, 'The Siting of Two Flintshire Paper Mills', *Industrial Archaeology,* Vol 2 No 4 (1965)

M. Chater, *Family Business: A History of Grosvenor Chater 1690-1977* (1977)

Printing

Every town in the area had its printing press by the early or mid-nineteenth century. Wrexham was the earliest; Richard Marsh became a bookseller in 1753, and published a number of books, mostly in Welsh, from 1772 onwards. In the nineteenth century, two notable firms were Hughes a'i Fab (Hughes & Son, established in 1820), who published the novels of Daniel Owen, and Woodall, Minshall & Thomas, who printed the historical works of A.N. Palmer. In Denbigh, Thomas Gee the elder acquired a printing business in 1813. His son, Thomas Gee (1815-98), who succeeded him, made the firm a national institution; he published a wide range of newspapers, magazines, dictionaries, and theological works, including an encyclopaedia, *Y Gwyddoniadur Cymreig,* and the newspaper *Baner ac Amserau Cymru.*

Ifano Jones, *Printing and Printers in Wales and Monmouthshire* (1925)

G.G. Lerry, 'The Industries of Denbighshire from Tudor Times to the Present Day: Part III . . . Printing and Publishing', *Denbs Hist Soc Trans,* Vol 9 (1960)

Making paper by hand at Afonwen, about 1900. The man in the distance is standing in front of a vat full of rag pulp. He dipped a flat, wire-meshed mould into the vat to form a sheet of paper; great skill was needed to distribute the pulp evenly. The mould was then passed to assistants, who turned the paper out onto a sheet of felt. Sheets of paper and felt were built up in alternate layers into a pile, which was then pressed to remove water. The paper was then dried, sized and hot-pressed to smooth it.

CROH *Photo 13/118*

Paper-makers at Afonwen, about 1900. The paper hats worn by some protected the hair from steam and size.

CROH Photo 13/71

Grosvenor Chater's Abbey Mills, Greenfield, about 1930.

CROH Photo 22/61

Oakenholt paper mill, about 1900.

CROH Photo 20/244

Paper-making machinery at Oakenholt, about 1900. Machinery for making paper was introduced into Britain from France, and improved by the brothers Fourdrinier, in the early years of the nineteenth century. Pulp flowed from a vat onto an endless belt of wire mesh, and the paper so made was pressed, dried and smoothed in a continuous process, and wound off the machine onto a reel at the other end. The operation took only two or three minutes, as opposed to a week or more by hand methods.

CROH Photo 20/260

The new paper mill at Shotton, 1985.

Thomas Gee with his employees, Denbigh, about 1890.

CROR Photo 24/86

Binding room of Hughes & Son, Wrexham, about 1910.

CROR Photo 101/262

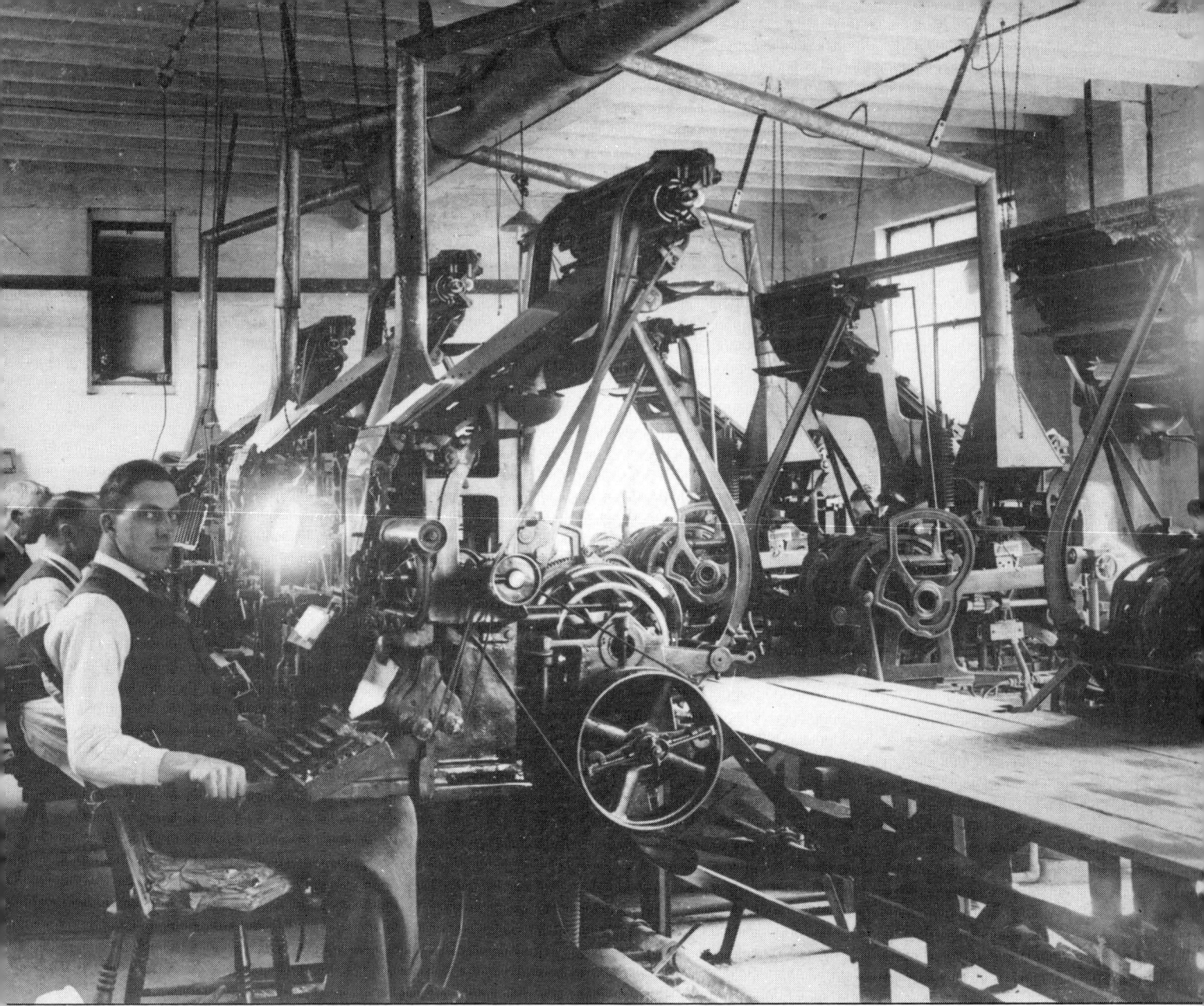

Type-setting, probably at Hughes & Son, about 1910. The linotype machine was invented in 1886, and its use spread rapidly, especially in newspaper offices. The operator sat at a keyboard similar to that of a typewriter, and assembled a line of type moulds; molten metal was then pumped in to cast a line of type.

CROR DD/GL/149

Leather

Tanyards were found in most towns up to the end of the ninteenth century, but Denbigh and Wrexham were the traditional centres of the leather industry. At Denbigh there were guilds of glovers and corvisors (shoe-makers) from as early as the sixteenth century. Denbigh specialized in the making of gloves, but there was also an important shoe-making industry. In 1790 the town had eight master glovers and breeches makers (leather breeches were supplied to the army), and eighteen boot and shoe makers. Shoes were sent to Liverpool, many of them for export to the West Indies and elsewhere. In 1810 about 7,000 dozen pairs of gloves were sent to London, Bristol and other towns. Boot and shoe leather was tanned locally, but the skins needed for glove-making came from Dolgellau. But these craft industries declined in the nineteenth century in the face of competition from factories (mostly in England) using improved machinery. By 1844 Denbigh was 'more a place of genteel retirement than trade'.

In Wrexham, like Denbigh a centre for the leather trade in the seventeenth and eighteenth centuries, the industry survived by turning to the manufacture of leather for the cotton industry, which required thin level-grown skins to cover the rollers in the spinning machinery invented by Richard Arkwright in 1769. Arkwright's former associate, John Smalley, established a cotton mill at Holywell in 1777. Soon afterwards he visited Wrexham fair and met John Peers, who in 1770 had founded a sheep-skin tannery in the town. As a result, Peers began to specialize in the production of roller leather, and supplied it not only to Holywell, but to the Lancashire mills. In 1822 a Montgomeryshire man, Evan Morris, succeeded to the business, and both improved the manufacturing processes and extended the works. The business was purchased in 1858 by two Wrexham men, J. Meredith Jones and Charles Rocke, who expanded to build the Cambrian Leather Works. Hand labour was largely replaced by machinery, much of it invented by Meredith Jones. The firm produced all kinds of leathers for the shoe and furniture trades, and specialized in supplying leather for bookbinding. It supplied most of the sheepskins used by the Cambridge University Press for the binding of the eleventh edition of *Encyclopaedia Britannica,* a contract involving nearly a million skins. The works closed about 1936.

G.G. Lerry, 'The Industries of Denbighshire from Tudor Times to the Present Day: Part III . . . Leather', *Denbs Hist Soc Trans,* Vol 8 (1959)
A. Seymour-Jones, *Roller Leather for Cotton Spinning* (1893)

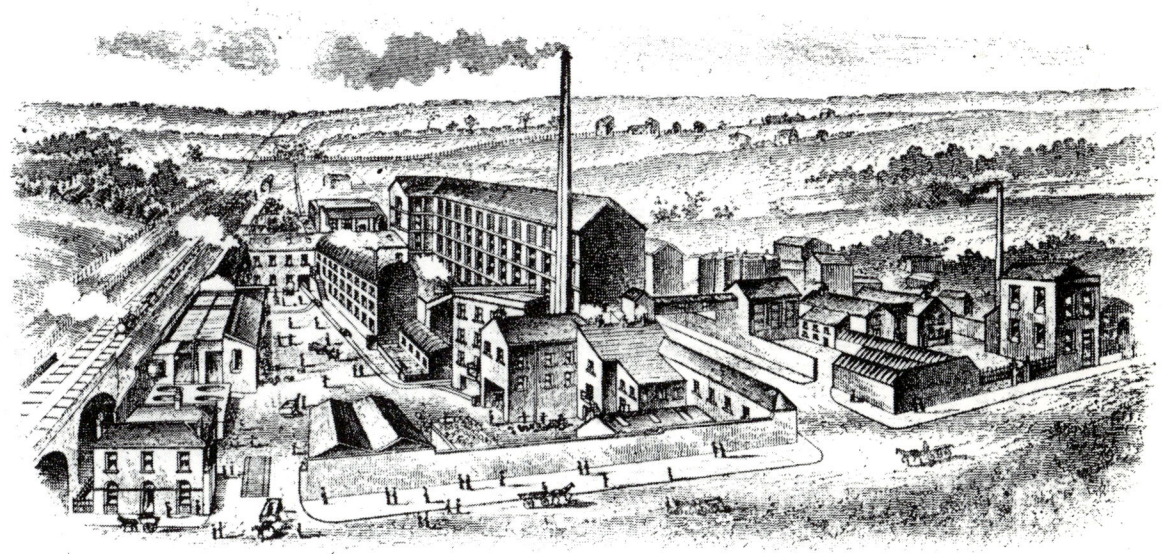

The Cambrian Leather Works, Wrexham, 1893.

A. Seymour-Jones, Roller Leather . . .*(1893)*

Glazing and ironing leather at the Cambrian works using agate and ironing with gas irons, about 1905.

CROR DD/DM/189

The Cambrian Leather Works, about 1910. The man on the extreme left is Alderman Edward Hughes of Glyndŵr, Wrexham, who was actively associated with the firm for many years.

CROR Glyndŵr MSS

Engineering

Bersham Ironworks in the late eighteenth century. Here John Wilkinson (see Iron and Steel) had machinery for boring cannnon; such was its accuracy that Wilkinson bored the cylinders for all the early steam engines made by Boulton and Watt. Examples of his work can be seen in this view of the west end of the works.

A.N. Palmer, John Wilkinson and the Old Bersham Iron Works *(1899)*

Sandycroft Foundry: general view from the firm's brochure, about 1908.

CROH D/DM/158/3

Sandycroft Foundry, 1907. The foundry came to Sandycroft, on the river Dee, in 1862. It made mining machinery and, from the 1890s, electric motors; it closed in 1925. The photograph shows a pair of winding engines made for an Indian gold mine.

CROH Photo 60/27

Willans & Robinson factory, Queensferry, about 1901. In 1899 Willans & Robinson Ltd of Rugby bought land on the river Dee and built a factory to manufacture water-tube boilers. The massive brick factory with its hydraulic accumulator tower, by the architect H.B. Creswell, dominated the area. The firm had a small steelworks where, in 1903, vanadium steel was first produced. Lack of orders forced the closure of the works in 1909. In 1914 German internees were housed in the factory until they were transferred to the Isle of Man, and in 1915 it became part of the Queensferry munitions factory (see War Factories).

CROH D/GL/91

Niclausse water-tube boiler under test at Queensferry. The boiler could attain full working pressure from cold water in half an hour, but proved to be expensive to produce. Willans & Robinson also made steam superheaters and feed-water heaters, as well as crankshafts and several types of gears in vanadium steel.

CROH D/GL/91

Wool washing machinery manufactured by Hughes & Lancaster, Acrefair, about 1920. The firm was founded in Chester in 1865, and moved to the former New British Iron Co works in Acrefair in 1891. Hughes & Lancaster made sewage ejectors and pumps, air compressors, and textile processing machinery. Textile machinery was supplied particularly to Yorkshire mills, but these and other products were exported all over the world. The works was acquired in 1951 by the Butterley Company, and later by Air Products Ltd (Acrefair Collection).

Employees of Henry Wood & Co, chainmakers, of Saltney. The firm, founded at Stourbridge in 1780, came to a new works on Boundary Lane, Saltney, in 1847. Woods had a world-wide reputation for manufacturing chain cables and anchors, and did much work for the Admiralty. The firm closed in 1964, when the premises were taken over by the Chester Chain Co. This photograph was taken when the king visited the works in 1917.

CROH Photo 58/26

Agricultural machinery made by John Williams & Son, Phoenix Ironworks, Rhuddlan, on display at an agricultural show, about 1910. These products, as well as oil engines for farmers, were made at this foundry from about 1860 to 1923.

CROH Photo 54/30

Shipbuilding

Shipbuilding in Chester probably dates from the medieval period, but the industry seems to have been stimulated by the building of the new cut of the river Dee in 1733-7. A number of small yards developed in the early nineteenth century on the south bank of the Dee and its estuary — at Sandycroft, Queensferry, Connah's Quay, Flint, Bagillt, Mostyn and Talacre. Most built schooners, sloops and flats, and few remained active after the 1860s.

George Cramm purchased a yard at Sandycroft in 1852, and there built the *Royal Charter,* the largest ship (2,719 tons) built on Deeside. He had difficulty launching the ship into the river; this may have weakened the vessel, which was wrecked off Anglesey with the loss of 439 lives when returning from Australia carrying gold bullion in 1859.

Of the larger yards which lasted into the twentieth century, Ferguson & Baird, established at Connah's Quay in 1872, built schooners. Their yard was taken over in 1920 by J. Crichton & Co, who also opened a yard at Saltney in 1913. The firm made a wide variety of vessels, including trawlers, tugs, paddle steamers, and floating grain elevators. Many were shallow-draught boats for operation on rivers in tropical countries. The yard was one of those bought up and closed in an attempt to rationalize the industry in 1935.

The Gloucestershire firm of Abdela & Mitchell began work at Queensferry in 1908. They built coasters, trawlers, barges and oil tankers, including several vessels (the *Carita* and the *Fleurita*) for John Summers & Sons. The last of the Dee shipyards, it closed in 1938.

Notes of George Lloyd, Shotton, on Dee shipyards (CROH D/GL/19,88,100)

D.P. Branigan, 'Estuary's Lost Shipyards', *Deesider* (July 1975)

D.P. Branigan, 'Shipbuilding on the River Dee', *Chester and the River Dee,* ed. Annette M. Kennett (Chester City Council, 1982)

Photograph albums, etc, of J. Crichton & Co, 1914-28 (CROH D/DM/338)

The Inde, *a passenger and cargo-carrying launch built at Crichton's for use at Calabar, Nigeria, 1924.*

CROH D/DM/338/3

Abdela & Mitchell's shipyard, Queensferry, about 1910.

CROH Photo 51/47

The Pepuhy, *the first boat built by Abdela & Mitchell at the re-opened*
Queensferry yard, about 1908.

CROH Photo 51/46

Construction of barges at Crichton's shipyard, Saltney, during the First World
War. Many of the workers are women.

CROH D/DM/338/3

Launch of the Isabeletta *at Crichton's, 1920. This three-masted steamer of 480 tons was built for J.H. Monks (Preston) Ltd for coasting service.*

CROH D/DM/338/3

Floating grain elevator built at Crichton's for use in the port of Liverpool, 1924.

CROH D/DM/338/3

Pottery, Bricks and Tiles

Buckley

Pottery was being made in the Buckley area in medieval times. By the late seventeenth century a small group of potters were working on Buckley Mountain, a suitable place on account of its supplies of clay and coal, with lead (for glazing) available nearby. Work was on a small scale, and high-quality pottery was produced. Since the difficulty of road transport made it preferable for pottery to be carried by water, the proximity of Buckley to the Dee estuary was an important factor. The canalization of the Dee in 1737 led to rapid growth in the industry.

In the late-eighteenth century, great quantities of functional products were produced for the kitchen and industrial purposes. The industry became dominated by two families, the Hancocks and Catheralls, to whom pottery was of lesser concern than brickmaking. In the early 1780s, when Thomas Pennant visited Buckley, he found fourteen potteries at work; they made between three and four thousand pounds worth of coarse earthenware a year, most of it being shipped to Ireland and the ports around the Welsh coast. Buckley black-glazed kitchen ware was in common use within reach of the area, and of the Welsh ports, until the twentieth century. In the last quarter of the nineteenth century the potteries, led by Powell's, turned to the making of art pottery until the end of production in 1940.

Apart from boulder clay used to make pottery, Buckley was rich in fireclay deposits suitable for brickmaking. Jonathan Catherall began to make bricks soon after the construction of the new Dee channel, and the industry developed rapidly, William Hancock being the other dominant manufacturer. Many works sprang up in the nineteenth century; the Castle Fire Brick Company was founded in 1865. Apart from bricks, these works produced other fireclay products such as tiles, pipes, chimney pots, etc. The area remained a brickmaking centre until contraction led to a series of closures in the 1960s and early 1970s.

J.E. Messham, 'The Buckley Pottery Industry', *Flints Hist Soc Jnl*, Vol 16 (1956)
Dennis Griffiths, *Out of this Clay* (1960)
J. Bentley, *A Short Account of the Buckley Potteries* (1982)
Buckley Pottery: The Craft and History of the Buckley Potters . . . (Mostyn Art Gallery exhibition catalogue, 1983)
Buckley — the magazine of the Buckley Society — contains numerous articles on the brick, tile and pottery industries.

Ruabon

The red marl of the Ruabon district made it an important centre for the making of bricks, tiles and terracotta in the late nineteenth and early twentieth centuries. These products were in great demand as new housing was built for the rising urban population. Ruabon brick was sent to all parts of Britain, and its distinctive red colour is a feature of the Wrexham and Ruabon areas in particular. The industry came to be dominated by two men, J.C. Edwards and Henry Dennis.

J.C. Edwards began to make bricks and tiles in a small way about 1860. He took over and expanded the Trefynant works, and in 1865 established the Penybont works, which made terracotta ware. Glazed and enamelled bricks were made at the Coppi, Rhos, and there was also a pottery at Plas Kynaston. Edwards specialized in the production of moulded terracotta and brightly-coloured tiles, both of which appealed strongly to late-Victorian tastes.

Henry Dennis, a Cornishman, established the Hafod brickworks by 1878, and built a new works on the firm's present site in 1893. Here tiles, bricks and terracotta were manufactured. Dennis's other works, Pant, made glazed bricks and sanitary ware. The Dennis works at Hafod is now the only representative of the Ruabon clay industries. In recent years a new production line has been built at a cost of £3.5 million, and the firm, which employs over 190 people, has about 60% of the UK market for quarry tiles.

G.G. Lerry, 'The Industries of Denbighshire from Tudor Times to the Present Day: Part III . . . Bricks and Tiles, Pottery', *Denbs Hist Soc Trans*, Vol 8 (1959)
Bricks, Tiles and Terracotta (Wrexham Maelor Borough Council exhibition catalogue, 1985)

Buckley potters at work — watercolour by Lady Delamere, 1823 (Sir William Gladstone).

CROH PR/F/106

Clayhole at the Belmont works of the Buckley Brick & Tile Co, 1894.

CROH Photo 11/215

The Castle Fire Brick Co works in the late-nineteenth century. The Old Works of the company, established in 1865, were on a siding of the Wrexham, Mold and Connah's Quay Railway. The company made both facing and silica bricks, and in 1916 was taken over by John Summers & Sons, who used its output at Shotton steelworks. In its later years the company took over a number of other brickworks in Buckley and elsewhere.

CROH D/DM/355/18

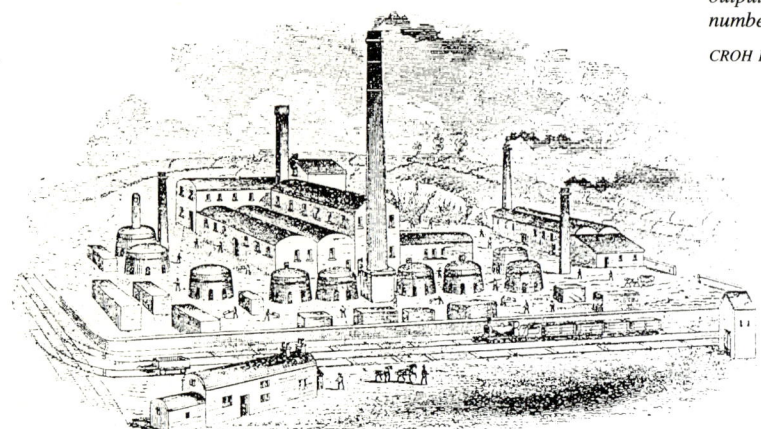

Workers in front of one of the kilns at Brookhill brickworks, 1894. The Buckley Brick & Tile Co, incorporated in 1865, operated two works, Brookhill and Belmont. The firm is associated with the Gibson family, two members of whom, John Philip Gibson and John Merriman Gibson, are standing at the extreme left and right of the main group. The firm was taken over by the Castle Brick Co in 1940, and closed in 1961.

CROH Photo 11/213

Dennis's Pant works, Rhos — a view from the firm's catalogue, 1908. The horse-drawn tramway on the right ran to the claypits, and the railway connected with the GWR Pontcysyllte branch.

CROR DD/DM/278/2

Hafod works of Dennis Ruabon, 1908. Sidings from the main GWR line in the background ran to the loading wharf behind the main building, and to Hafod Colliery and coke works to the right.

CROR DD/DM/278/2

Brick-making press at J.C. Edwards's works, about 1910 (Acrefair Collection).

CROR Photo 16/19

J.C. Edwards's Trefynant works, Acrefair, 1954 (Acrefair Collection).

Oil

A sizeable oil industry developed in the 1860s in the Leeswood, Coed Talon and Padeswood areas, and at Acrefair. Here, as in other colliery districts in Britain, crude oil was distilled in retorts from cannel coal and shales. Slater's *Directory* listed no less than twenty-two mineral oil manufacturers in the Mold area alone in 1868. The crude oil was sent for further refining to works at Saltney, Queensferry and Bagillt. It was oil which brought the chemist, R.F. Graesser, to Acrefair in 1867 (see Chemicals). The industry collapsed after 1870 with the opening up of the great oilfields in the United States, and the resulting rapid fall in prices.

Oil is back in the news, however, with the building of a pilot plant to produce oil from coal at Point of Ayr (see Coal), and drilling for oil on the Cheshire-Clwyd border, and in Liverpool Bay.

H. Gregory, 'The Distillation of Oil from Cannel Coal and Shales', *Flints Hist Soc Jnl,* Vol 25 (1971-2)

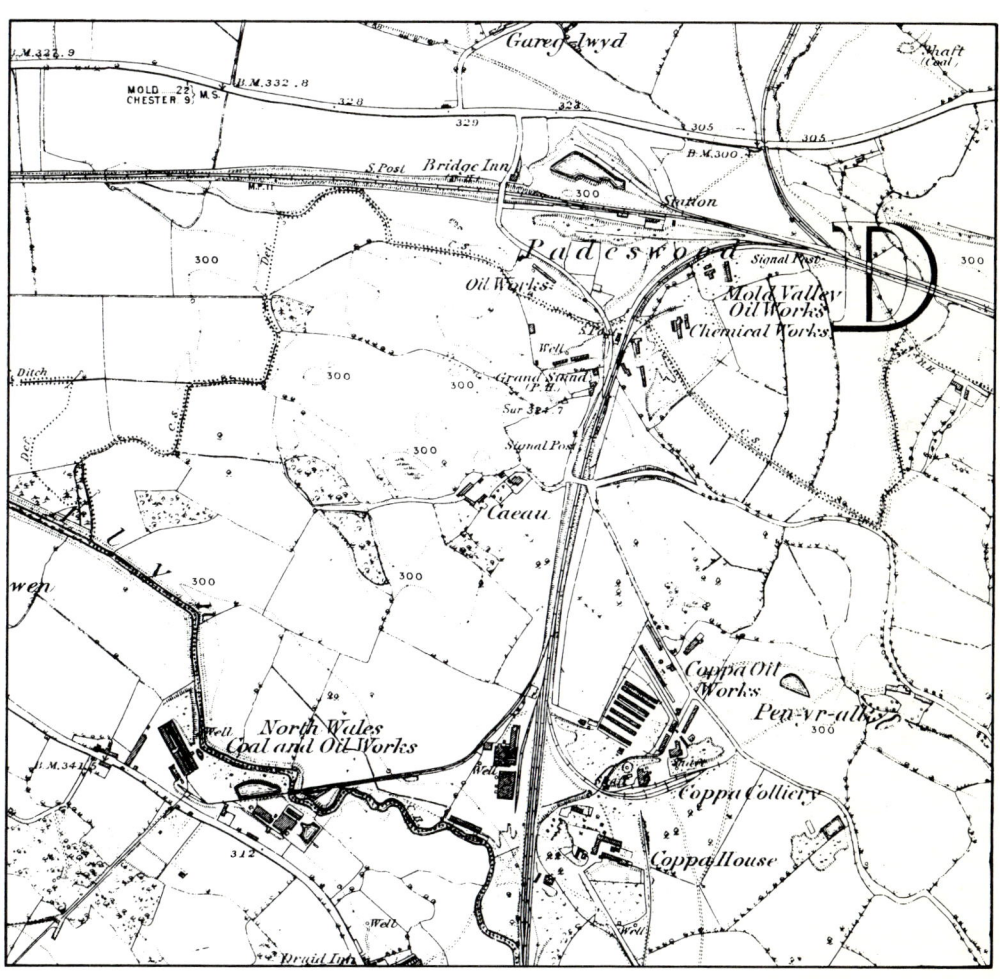

Ordnance Survey 6-inch map showing oil works in the Padeswood area, 1870.

Rope

Wrexham rope-walk, 1854. Rope walks were established in or near the larger towns to supply the great quantities of rope needed in ships and in lead and coal mines. Pigot's Directory, 1835, *recorded ropemakers in Denbigh, Bagillt and Holywell, and two in Wrexham. This billhead of Robert Davies of Hope Street, Wrexham, shows the rope-making process. A spinner with a bundle of hemp around his waist attached the fibres to a hook on a whirl, driven by a large wheel turned by an assistant. The spinner, who covered many miles in the course of a day's work, walked backwards down the walk, paying out more fibres to form yarn. When he reached the end of the walk, his assistant took the yarn off the hook and reeled it in as the spinner walked forwards. The process was repeated as yarns were twisted into strands, and strands into ropes, partially completed ropes being hooked out of the way overhead.*

The bill, to the churchwardens of Gresford, was for bell-ropes for Gresford and Rossett churches.

CROR PD/34/1/174

War Factories

In both world wars, the desperate need for munitions led to the building of large numbers of new factories, most of which were closed down again with the ending of hostilities. In the First World War, a big explosives factory was established at Queensferry, and shells were made at Wrexham. The Queensferry factory, built in 1915, manufactured guncotton and TNT. At its peak it employed 7,300 people, nearly half of them women, who were brought in by train and bus from a wide area of Flintshire, Denbighshire and Cheshire. It closed in 1918.

At the end of the Second World War there were forty-four Royal Ordnance Factories in Britain, of which only three were in existence in 1937. Three categories of factory were built — engineering, explosives and filling. The explosives factory at Marchwiel, Wrexham, covering 1,400 acres and employing some 4,000 workers, came into production in February 1941, just over a year from the start of construction. At Rhydymwyn, ROF Valley filled shells with poison gas brought by rail from the ICI plant at Runcorn. Here also,

in 1942-3, ICI operated a model plant for the separation of uranium by the gaseous diffusion method, in connection with the atomic bomb project.

The aircraft factory at Broughton (see Aircraft) was built as a shadow factory to make bombers in 1937-9. There were other, smaller factories. At Ruthin, the Lang Pen Co took over the old county gaol to make shell parts. Production at the steelworks at Shotton and Brymbo was also stimulated by the need to make steel for the war effort.

H.M. Factory, Queensferry: Its History and Development . . .(1918)
Ian Hay, *ROF* (1948)
W. Hornby, *Factories and Plant* (History of the Second World War, Civil Series, 1958)
Margaret Gowing, *Britain and Atomic Energy 1939-45* (1964)

Women munition workers in Wrexham during the First World War. The war brought women into many industries for the first time.

CROR Photo 101/311

Manufacture of howitzer bombs at Powell Bros & Whitaker's Cambrian Ironworks, Wrexham, about 1915. The firm, who made agricultural machinery, turned in the First World War to munitions, producing some 10,000 shells and 1,500 howitzer bombs a week. About a hundred women were employed on this work.

CROR DD/DM/543/25

Queensferry Factory, about 1915. The photograph shows the partially-completed works, which covered some 300 acres on each side of the main Chester to Holyhead railway line.

CROH Photo 51/97

Making shell parts in the old gaol at Ruthin, about 1942. The building now houses the Ruthin branch of the Clwyd Record Office.

CROR Photo 90/265

Aircraft

The only aircraft manufacturing plant in Wales is at Broughton — the British Aerospace Chester factory. This was one of a number of government-built shadow factories for large-scale aircraft production. Work on it began in late 1937, and the first aircraft was completed in August 1939. The factory was managed for the government by Vickers-Armstrong. During the war, Vickers built 5,540 Wellington bombers, most of them at Broughton, and 235 Lancaster bombers were made in 1944-5. At its peak production, 130 Wellingtons were built in a month, and 6,000 workers, half of them women, were employed. On a famous occasion in 1944, a complete Wellington was built in just over twenty-four hours. The factory shared the airfield with RAF Hawarden, at which, in 1940-2, an officer training unit instructed Spitfire pilots.

At the end of the war, the factory turned to production of prefabricated aluminium houses, better known as 'pre-fabs', of which over 28,000 were made in 1945-8. These were intended as a temporary solution to the severe housing shortage, but many are still in fact inhabited to this day.

Aircraft were again built from 1948, when de Havillands took over the factory to make Mosquitoes, Hornets, Doves and Vampires. Other types built included early Comets. In 1963, under the reorganization of the aircraft industry, de Havilland become part of Hawker-Siddeley. In the previous year the first 125 executive jet was built. Orders for it continue to keep the factory (now part of British Aerospace) busy, together with wings for the European Airbus.

D.J. Smith, *Hawarden: A Welsh Airfield 1939-1979* (1979)
D.J. Smith, *Action Stations 3: Military Airfields of Wales and the North-West* (1981)
Wings [Newsletter of British Aerospace, Chester], Nos 3-4 (1979)

Wellington R1333 at Broughton, 1940. £15,000 was raised by employees to pay for this aircraft, but on 14 November 1940, a week after the photograph was taken, it was damaged in an air raid on the factory, and subsequently written off. The raid may have been a diversion from the Luftwaffe attack on Coventry, which took place on the same night.

CROH Photo 9/35

Lancaster bombers under construction at Broughton (British Aerospace).

CROH Photo 9/42

Work on early 125s at Broughton, 1963 (British Aerospace).

CROH Photo 9/43

New Industries

Clwyd has a long tradition of major industrial development, with an economic base centred upon a narrow range of staple industries which were large employers: steel-making, coal-mining and textile manufacture. The last ten years have seen a rapid decline in these sectors as significant employers, but diversification of the economy is now taking place. Industrial regeneration is the foremost priority of the county and district councils, and the other public agencies involved in this important task. The changes in employment patterns have resulted in a large pool of labour being available, and in addition, as a result of the rapid growth in the county's population during the 1960s and 1970s, large numbers of young people are entering the labour market each year.

Major companies have moved into the area to take advantage of this large pool of labour. Soon after the war, the area east of Wrexham which had been a Royal Ordnance Factory became a trading estate (now the Wrexham Industrial Estate), and new industries have been attracted to this and other sites. A great deal of industrial land is being developed — over 1,000 acres on the Deeside Industrial Park, 600 on the Wrexham Industrial Estate, 290 on the Delyn Enterprise Zone at Flint, and more at smaller locations. The attractions of Clwyd are many. Grant aid is readily available, for the eastern half of the county is a Development Area, and the county is designated a Steel and Coal Closure Area. Clwyd is situated near to the centre of Britain, and fifteen million people live within a two hours' radius. The area has a skilled workforce, with an excellent industrial relations record; housing is relatively cheap and educational standards high.

Between 1981 and the end of 1984 some 250 companies were attracted to Clwyd, creating 5,000 jobs. The new industries established include well-known concerns such as Pilkington, Kelloggs, Hotpoint, Laura Ashley, Kimberley-Clark and Cadbury's. Brother, a major Japanese manufacturer of electronic goods such as typewriters, has opened a new plant near Wrexham, and the Sharp Corporation of Japan is making video recorders at Llay. TetraPak is expanding its packaging factory at Wrexham. At Shotton, Deeside Titanium has been set up by a group of major companies, and United Paper Mills of Finland has invested in a new paper mill.

Significantly, the regeneration of the local economy has produced a wide range of companies operating in areas of new technology. Clwyd has proved to be a highly attractive location for companies such as Optical Fibres (BICC and Corning Glass), Remsdaq, Burroughs, Metal Improvement Company (Curtis Wright), Squibb Surgicare and Data Magnetics.

For science and technology based industries, the role of the North-East Wales Institute of Higher Education is of a vital catalyst. The institute, with major campuses at Deeside and Wrexham, offers a wide range of courses up to degree level and a whole range of industrial subjects including electronics, computing, micro-electronics, robotics and bio-technology. Recognizing the need for research and innovative support, the county council and the North-East Wales Institute, with the support of the Welsh Development Agency, have established a research and innovation centre on Deeside Industrial Park called Newtech. The services of Newtech are available for research and development consultancy and for training services.

At the same time, smaller concerns have not been neglected. The county has built more than fifty starter units for new businesses. A healthy growth of medium-sized enterprises will assist the diversification of the county's economy.

Clwyd Connection (Economic Development News from Clwyd County Council, 1985-)
Clwyd County Council Official Guide (1986)

Clwyd's Industrial Past

Industrial Documents

The County Archivist is anxious to preserve documents and photographs relating to the county's industrial past. Many industrial records have already been deposited in the record office for safe-keeping, and the illustrations selected from the photographic collection for inclusion in this volume are evidence of the wealth of such material already available. However, much remains in private hands, and should be preserved. Anyone knowing of such material is requested to contact the County Archivist, Clwyd Record Office, The Old Rectory, Hawarden. Tel: Hawarden (0244) 532364.

Historical Societies

The county historical societies publish journals which include much on industrial history, and also organize lectures, day schools, and field excursions. The secretaries are:

Denbighshire: W.C. Wynne-Woodhouse, Gorffwysfa, Llansannan, Denbigh. Tel: Llansannan (074 577) 386.
Flintshire: Mrs I.M. Read, 50 Hafod Park, Mold. Tel: Mold (0352) 2582.

Bersham Industrial Heritage Centre

The centre, run by Clwyd County Council, is situated on the Bersham and Clywedog Industrial Trail, which runs from Minera to King's Mills, Wrexham. This is an eight-mile long open-air museum which reflects industrial activity in the Clywedog valley from Roman times to the present day. The centre itself provides permanent exhibitions, the main ones being on John Wilkinson and the Bersham Ironworks, and on the Davies brothers, gatesmiths of Croes Foel. Temporary exhibitions are also displayed regularly. Further information is available from the Curator, Bersham Industrial Heritage Centre, Bersham, Wrexham. Tel: Wrexham (0978) 261529.

Greenfield Valley Visitor Centre

The water which flows from St Winefride's Well, at Holywell, runs for one and a half miles down the Greenfield Valley, past historic Basingwerk Abbey to the river Dee. This water power made the valley an important centre for many industries, and Thomas Williams, the Copper King, set up copper and brass works in the late eighteenth century. Today relics of this past may be seen in the reservoirs and remains of industrial buildings. Delyn Borough Council's Visitor Centre has a permanent exhibition on the history of the valley, and at Abbey Farm there is a large display of farming tools and machinery, as well as a growing collection of animals. Further information is available from the Visitor Centre, Greenfield Valley, Holywell. Tel: Holywell (0352) 714172.

. . . and Future

The Economic Development Division

Economic regeneration is Clwyd County Council's first priority, and its Economic Development Division operates an energetic marketing campaign to attract new industrial investment to Clwyd from both the UK and overseas. In partnership with the Welsh Development Agency, the Welsh Office and other local authorities the division offers a comprehensive and confidential service to companies seeking to invest in Clwyd. For further information contact Derek Griffin, County Economic Development Officer, Shire Hall, Mold. Tel: Mold (0352) 2121.